Keto Diet Cookbook For Women Over 50

Your Beginner's Guide To Having Your Dream Body After Fifty.
Follow A 30-Day Meal Plan With Easy, Tasty,
Low-Cost Recipes To Lose Weight
And Feel Great.

TIFFANY GRANT

TABLE OF CONTENTS

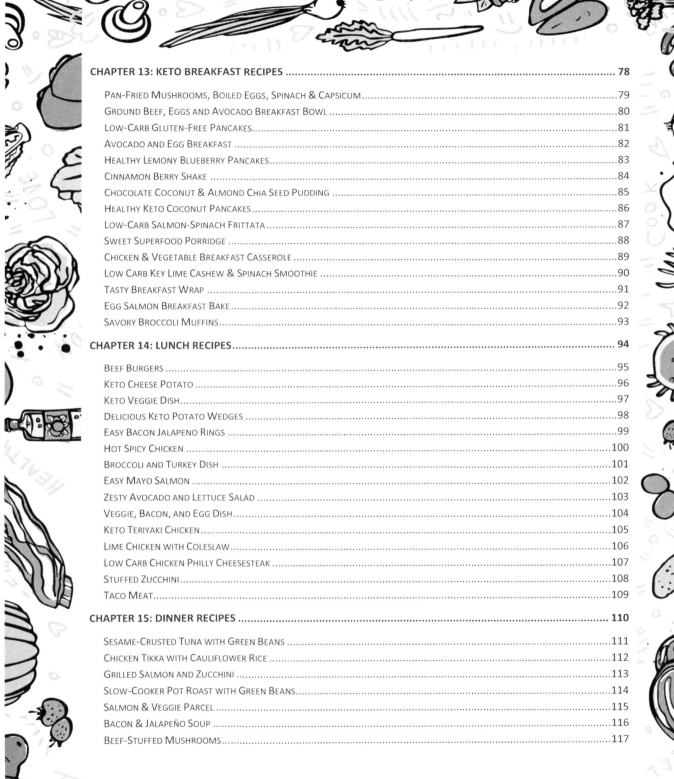

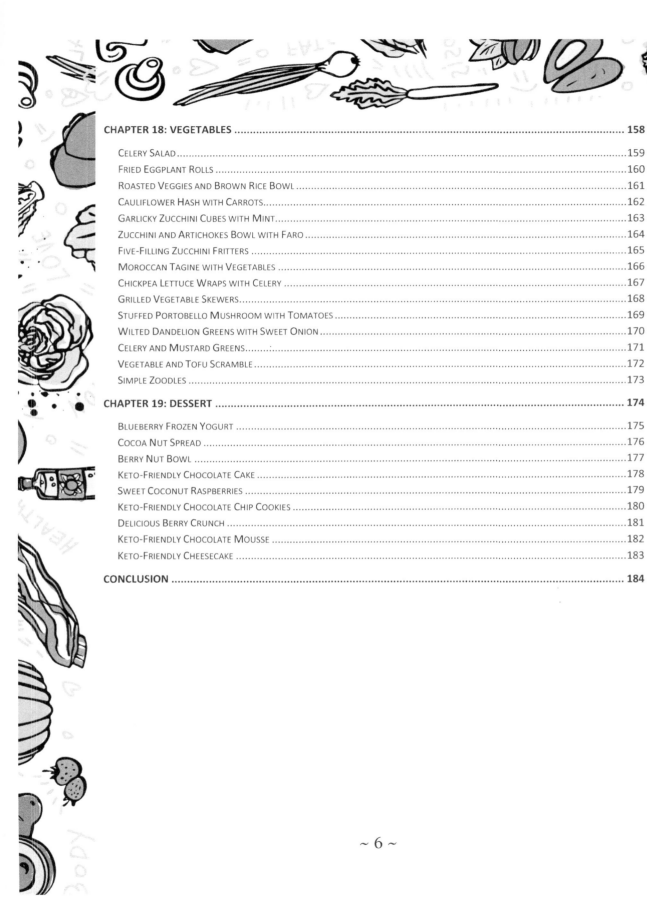

DESCRIPTION

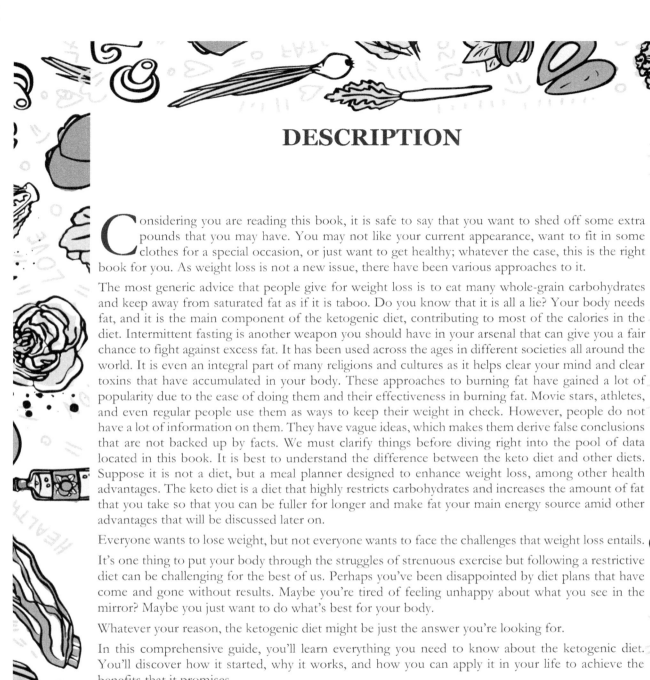

Considering you are reading this book, it is safe to say that you want to shed off some extra pounds that you may have. You may not like your current appearance, want to fit in some clothes for a special occasion, or just want to get healthy; whatever the case, this is the right book for you. As weight loss is not a new issue, there have been various approaches to it.

The most generic advice that people give for weight loss is to eat many whole-grain carbohydrates and keep away from saturated fat as if it is taboo. Do you know that it is all a lie? Your body needs fat, and it is the main component of the ketogenic diet, contributing to most of the calories in the diet. Intermittent fasting is another weapon you should have in your arsenal that can give you a fair chance to fight against excess fat. It has been used across the ages in different societies all around the world. It is even an integral part of many religions and cultures as it helps clear your mind and clear toxins that have accumulated in your body. These approaches to burning fat have gained a lot of popularity due to the ease of doing them and their effectiveness in burning fat. Movie stars, athletes, and even regular people use them as ways to keep their weight in check. However, people do not have a lot of information on them. They have vague ideas, which makes them derive false conclusions that are not backed up by facts. We must clarify things before diving right into the pool of data located in this book. It is best to understand the difference between the keto diet and other diets. Suppose it is not a diet, but a meal planner designed to enhance weight loss, among other health advantages. The keto diet is a diet that highly restricts carbohydrates and increases the amount of fat that you take so that you can be fuller for longer and make fat your main energy source amid other advantages that will be discussed later on.

Everyone wants to lose weight, but not everyone wants to face the challenges that weight loss entails.

It's one thing to put your body through the struggles of strenuous exercise but following a restrictive diet can be challenging for the best of us. Perhaps you've been disappointed by diet plans that have come and gone without results. Maybe you're tired of feeling unhappy about what you see in the mirror? Maybe you just want to do what's best for your body.

Whatever your reason, the ketogenic diet might be just the answer you're looking for.

In this comprehensive guide, you'll learn everything you need to know about the ketogenic diet. You'll discover how it started, why it works, and how you can apply it in your life to achieve the benefits that it promises.

You can overcome these severe problems just by intermittent fasting. It is not as if problems don't have their solutions. Solutions do exist. It depends on you if you are willing enough to convert your problem to your advantage. Intermittent fasting is not as if you fast. You only schedule your eating habits. You only eat when the right time is there. You do not eat 24/7. That is the root of obesity. Constant snacking slacks you from your life.

INTRODUCTION

A ketogenic diet is a high fat, moderate protein, and low-carbohydrate diet that can effectively lose weight and improve your lifestyle.

A "ketogenic" essentially describes the increased production of ketone systems occasioned by the heightened price of lipolysis. Ketones are the acid byproducts created when the liver breaks down "fats" into "fatty acids."

Nowadays, the promoters of ketogenic diet programs are clear that carbohydrates mainly increase the glycemic index, so individuals put on weight.

Foods containing carbohydrates are usually metabolized to create a kind of basic sugar, which is frequently considered the body's ideal energy source.

Among the macronutrients, carbs are thus considered to be the main reason for fat intake. This is especially true since the increased consumption of high glycemic index foods typically leads to fluctuations in blood glucose levels due to their rapid absorption directly into the bloodstream, which often results in an overproduction of insulin. Here is where the issue starts.

Insulin is the hormone that regulates blood sugar levels and the energy balance of the body. Excessive quantities of sugar in the bloodstream will cause the substantial secretion of insulin, resulting in the storage of the surplus sugar within the body as both glycogens for muscle and liver cells or extra fat in fat cells.

A goal of ketogenic diet programs is to reduce insulin generation to the barest minimum by substantially reducing carbohydrate usage while using proteins and fats to augment the body's energy requirement. Regardless of ketogenic diet programs' capability to decrease insulin generation, the main objective is eventually targeted at inducing ketosis.

Ketosis is another status of lipolysis (fat break down), and it is a metabolic process in which the body burns stored fat for energy instead of glucose. Ketogenic diet programs are thus favorably disposed to the support and promotion of ketosis.

Extended periods of fasting can be induced naturally. However, it can also be caused intentionally by using a low-carbohydrate or low-calorie diet regime to absorb considerable amounts of either fat or protein-rich foods and radically reduced carbohydrates.

Thus, high-protein and high-fat diets are weight loss diets used to induce ketosis.

CHAPTER 1:

WHAT IS THE KETO DIET ALL ABOUT? AND HOW DOES IT WORK?

Keto diet consists of low-carb and high-fat food items that directly force our body to burn all the fat for body energy in place of sugar and carbs. The keto diet forces our body to use up the stored fat, which allows the body's fat cells to release all the fatty acids. The fatty acids, in turn, get converted into ketones by the liver. As the process starts, the body gets into the state of ketosis, where ketones are burnt down for energy instead of sugar or glucose. As the overall intake of carbs gets reduced in this form of the diet, the ketones turn out to be the main energy source. This ultimately results in a significant amount of weight loss.

A ketogenic diet is something that you should start today for a better lifestyle if you are over 50. The ketogenic diet is more common in women than in men because of all the benefits it provides for dealing with the symptoms of menopause. Women who are experiencing menopause, or have already experienced it, have a clear idea of the troubles that come along with it. Menopause leads to fatigue, irritability and also increases weight. But the keto diet can help in controlling your body weight and also improve your physical wellbeing. Not sure how to start with keto?

As the diet continues to grow in popularity, more research is being performed on the ketogenic diet by the day! With science-backed evidence, you can follow the diet and know for a fact that it is going to work. Welcome to your first ketogenic diet science lesson! One of the best parts of the ketogenic diet is that it is based on a natural process that your body already has!

Overall, the fuel that we use the most is stored as triglyceride in our adipose tissue, aka, fat! The second most used source is protein and glucose, used depending upon your body's metabolic state.

So, what determines what fuel to use and when? As you might have already guessed, the primary determinant is based upon carbohydrate availability. Additional factors that can affect fuel utilization include a full or empty liver glycogen level and certain enzyme levels.

These three different storage depots include protein, carbohydrates, and fats! Protein is essential in your diet because it can be converted into glucose in your liver and used as energy. Carbohydrates are typically stored as glycogen and are placed in your liver and muscle. On the other hand, fat is generally stored as body fat, but we will get to that in a second.

When you follow a SAD diet (or a Standard American Diet), ketones truly have a non-existent role in your energy production. However, as you begin a ketogenic diet, it will play a much more significant role, and here we introduce the fourth potential fuel source for your body! As you start to decrease the carbohydrate availability through diet, your body will automatically shift to using fat as your first fuel source.

How the Ketogenic Diet Works

Before we talk about how to do keto, it's important first to consider why this particular diet works. What happens to your body to make you lose weight?

As you probably know, the body uses food as an energy source. Everything you eat is turned into energy so that you can get up and do whatever you need to accomplish for the day. The main energy source is sugar, so what happens is that you eat something, the body breaks it down into sugar, and the sugar is processed into energy. Typically, the "sugar" is taken directly from the food you eat, so

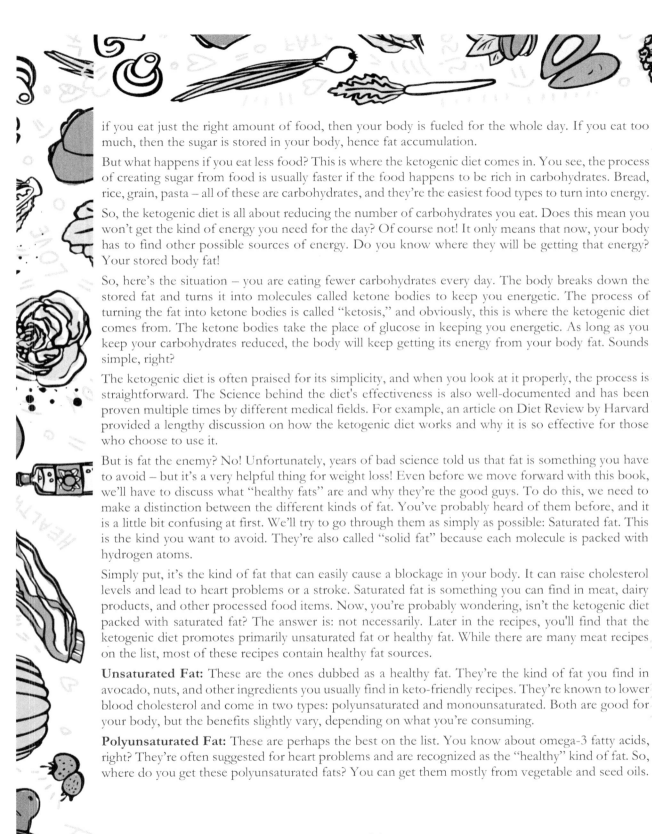

if you eat just the right amount of food, then your body is fueled for the whole day. If you eat too much, then the sugar is stored in your body, hence fat accumulation.

But what happens if you eat less food? This is where the ketogenic diet comes in. You see, the process of creating sugar from food is usually faster if the food happens to be rich in carbohydrates. Bread, rice, grain, pasta – all of these are carbohydrates, and they're the easiest food types to turn into energy.

So, the ketogenic diet is all about reducing the number of carbohydrates you eat. Does this mean you won't get the kind of energy you need for the day? Of course not! It only means that now, your body has to find other possible sources of energy. Do you know where they will be getting that energy? Your stored body fat!

So, here's the situation – you are eating fewer carbohydrates every day. The body breaks down the stored fat and turns it into molecules called ketone bodies to keep you energetic. The process of turning the fat into ketone bodies is called "ketosis," and obviously, this is where the ketogenic diet comes from. The ketone bodies take the place of glucose in keeping you energetic. As long as you keep your carbohydrates reduced, the body will keep getting its energy from your body fat. Sounds simple, right?

The ketogenic diet is often praised for its simplicity, and when you look at it properly, the process is straightforward. The Science behind the diet's effectiveness is also well-documented and has been proven multiple times by different medical fields. For example, an article on Diet Review by Harvard provided a lengthy discussion on how the ketogenic diet works and why it is so effective for those who choose to use it.

But is fat the enemy? No! Unfortunately, years of bad science told us that fat is something you have to avoid – but it's a very helpful thing for weight loss! Even before we move forward with this book, we'll have to discuss what "healthy fats" are and why they're the good guys. To do this, we need to make a distinction between the different kinds of fat. You've probably heard of them before, and it is a little bit confusing at first. We'll try to go through them as simply as possible: Saturated fat. This is the kind you want to avoid. They're also called "solid fat" because each molecule is packed with hydrogen atoms.

Simply put, it's the kind of fat that can easily cause a blockage in your body. It can raise cholesterol levels and lead to heart problems or a stroke. Saturated fat is something you can find in meat, dairy products, and other processed food items. Now, you're probably wondering, isn't the ketogenic diet packed with saturated fat? The answer is: not necessarily. Later in the recipes, you'll find that the ketogenic diet promotes primarily unsaturated fat or healthy fat. While there are many meat recipes on the list, most of these recipes contain healthy fat sources.

Unsaturated Fat: These are the ones dubbed as a healthy fat. They're the kind of fat you find in avocado, nuts, and other ingredients you usually find in keto-friendly recipes. They're known to lower blood cholesterol and come in two types: polyunsaturated and monounsaturated. Both are good for your body, but the benefits slightly vary, depending on what you're consuming.

Polyunsaturated Fat: These are perhaps the best on the list. You know about omega-3 fatty acids, right? They're often suggested for heart problems and are recognized as the "healthy" kind of fat. So, where do you get these polyunsaturated fats? You can get them mostly from vegetable and seed oils.

You can almost always find these ingredients in Ketogenic Recipes, such as olive oil, coconut oil, and more. If you need more convincing, you should also know that omega-3 fatty acids are a kind of polyunsaturated fats, and you will find them in deep-sea fish like tuna, herring, and salmon.

CHAPTER 2:

THE SCIENCE BEHIND THE KETO DIET

Turning 50 is a big milestone in your life, and it brings about many changes, both in your family life and to your body physically. Maybe your children have left the house to go to college or to settle down and start their own family, and you find that you have more time on your hands than you know what to do with. Or maybe you have noticed that your hair is turning grey at a faster rate, that your eyesight and hearing are no longer what they used to be, and that you have aches and pains that you never had before.

Turning 50 is different for everyone. You might be excited to start a new adventure, or you are not prepared and are dreading the coming changes. But no matter what your take on turning 50 is, you cannot stop it from happening. So, now is the time to take control of your life, eat healthy food, lose weight, and prepare your body for the next stage of your life so that you can face everything that comes your way with confidence and grace.

Here are some of the changes you will be experiencing as you turn 50 or over:

Your metabolism slows down

Even before you turn 50, you might have noticed that your metabolism has started to slow down. However, at 50 and over, this becomes more noticeable than before. You might find that you are gaining weight from eating the same foods that you ate when you were younger to maintain your weight. This means that as you get older and your metabolism slows down, you should eat smaller food portions if you want to maintain the same weight as before and eat significantly less than that if you want to lose weight.

Your bones become brittle

When your body goes through menopause and your estrogen levels decrease, the rate at which your bones deteriorate increases, making your bones more brittle. You must begin strength training to keep you strong and prevent further bone loss, resulting in injuries.

Your muscles will become weaker

The rate at which you lose muscle mass is another factor affected by menopause when hormones like estrogen are reduced in your body. When you experience muscle loss, your muscles will become weaker. I suggest that you include endurance training, such as lifting weights and high-intensity interval training, to continue to strengthen your muscles.

You may experience problems with your digestive system

As you go through menopause and post menopause, your body and hormones will change. When your metabolism slows down, and your muscles become weaker, your stomach muscles will struggle to digest some foods, such as dairy and gluten. As a result, you will experience problems with your digestive system like bloating or constipation. If you are experiencing digestive issues, you should cut out foods one at a time to see which one is causing your stomach problems.

Once you have identified the culprit, you can either try and avoid eating it, if, for example, you have become lactose intolerant, or eat the problem food in smaller amounts so that you can reduce your chances of developing digestion problems.

You will struggle to lose weight

When you get older and your metabolism slows down, you will notice that you cannot lose weight as effectively as you used to. This is because as we get older, our bodies struggle to convert fat into energy that can then be used throughout the day, especially when you are including other energy sources in your diet as carbs. As a result, your body will retain the fat you consume, and you will struggle to lose it.

You may develop arthritis

If you have someone in your family who has arthritis, then there is an increased chance that you will develop it in your 50s or older. By staying active and exercising, you could decrease your symptoms and reduce any inflammation and pain that you may experience. By keeping your body moving, you could reduce the risk of having an arthritis attack.

Your body will struggle to produce protein

As you get older, you will need to consume more protein because your body will no longer produce and retain the protein. When you do not include enough protein in your diet, you can experience muscle loss and weakness. By including more protein in your diet, you will be able to maintain your muscle mass for longer.

Your brain function may weaken

If you do not continuously learn new things and exercise your brain, your brain function could deteriorate. When your brain function weakens, you could have trouble remembering things or develop memory loss, and your attention span could decrease. You can continue to exercise your brain and develop your brain function by breaking your daily routine and doing something out of the ordinary, meeting new people, and experiencing new events and locations.

What Nutrients Does My Body Need at 50?

Once you are aware of the changes that you might experience at 50 and over, you should find out more about what nutrients your body needs and be sure to include them in your diet. Below I have listed some of the main nutrients that will benefit your diet as you get older.

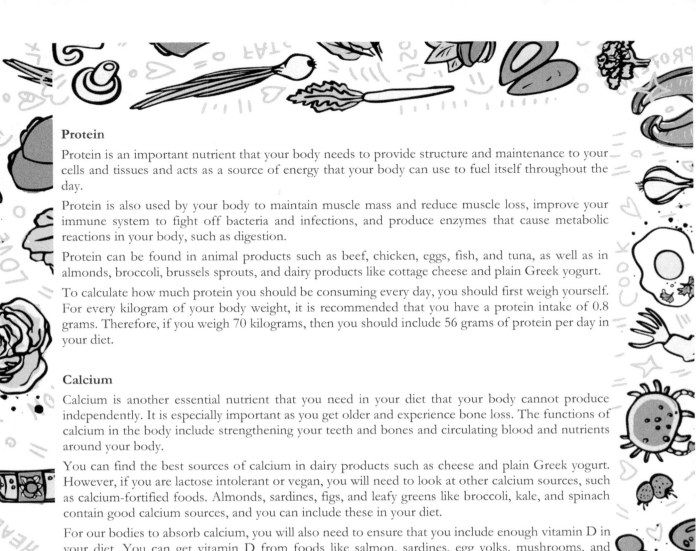

Protein

Protein is an important nutrient that your body needs to provide structure and maintenance to your cells and tissues and acts as a source of energy that your body can use to fuel itself throughout the day.

Protein is also used by your body to maintain muscle mass and reduce muscle loss, improve your immune system to fight off bacteria and infections, and produce enzymes that cause metabolic reactions in your body, such as digestion.

Protein can be found in animal products such as beef, chicken, eggs, fish, and tuna, as well as in almonds, broccoli, brussels sprouts, and dairy products like cottage cheese and plain Greek yogurt.

To calculate how much protein you should be consuming every day, you should first weigh yourself. For every kilogram of your body weight, it is recommended that you have a protein intake of 0.8 grams. Therefore, if you weigh 70 kilograms, then you should include 56 grams of protein per day in your diet.

Calcium

Calcium is another essential nutrient that you need in your diet that your body cannot produce independently. It is especially important as you get older and experience bone loss. The functions of calcium in the body include strengthening your teeth and bones and circulating blood and nutrients around your body.

You can find the best sources of calcium in dairy products such as cheese and plain Greek yogurt. However, if you are lactose intolerant or vegan, you will need to look at other calcium sources, such as calcium-fortified foods. Almonds, sardines, figs, and leafy greens like broccoli, kale, and spinach contain good calcium sources, and you can include these in your diet.

For our bodies to absorb calcium, you will also need to ensure that you include enough vitamin D in your diet. You can get vitamin D from foods like salmon, sardines, egg yolks, mushrooms, and fortified foods with vitamin D added to them. Sunlight also provides you with a natural source of vitamin D.

At the age of 50 should take 1,000 mg of calcium and 600 IU of vitamin D in their diet every day. Meanwhile, women over the age of 51 should increase their calcium intake to 1,200 mg, and women over the age of 70 should increase their daily vitamin D intake. You can take a calcium supplement if you are struggling to include the recommended amount in your diet.

Fiber

Fiber is a nutrient that improves your metabolism, digest the food you eat, keep your bowel movements regular, lose weight, and keep your blood sugar levels steady. Fiber can be a beneficial nutrient to consume in your diet and help improve health conditions like diabetes.

Food sources that are sources of fiber include all leafy greens, such as broccoli, brussels sprouts, lettuce, avocado, tomato, some berries, nuts like almonds, walnuts, and seeds like chia, flax, and hemp.

It is recommended that you include 25 grams of fiber every day in your diet. I suggest that you include a fiber supplement for the first few days if you are changing your diet to help you remain regular as your body gets used to the new foods.

Vitamin B12

Vitamin B12 is an essential nutrient that you should include in your diet. It helps to strengthen your brain function and keeps it from deteriorating as you get older, and it helps to produce oxygenated red blood cells that are transported through your body.

Vitamin B12 is found in animal products such as dairy, beef, chicken, eggs, and fish. If you are a vegetarian or vegan, vitamin B12 will be harder to include in your diet, but some fortified food alternatives, such as dairy, that you can use that have vitamin B12 added.

After 50, you have a greater risk of developing a vitamin B12 deficiency, which can be dangerous to your health. Suppose there is concern that you are not receiving enough vitamin B12 in your diet. In that case, it is recommended that you consider taking a vitamin B12 supplement and including fortified food alternatives in your diet.

It is recommended that if you are over the age of 50, you should take 500 mcg of vitamin B12 each day and up to 1,000 mcg in more severe cases of deficiency.

Potassium

Potassium is a nutrient that you should include in your diet that helps your body function properly by improving digestion, stabilizing your blood pressure, improving the signals transmitted along nerves in your body, and reducing your risk of osteoporosis and stroke.

You can also use potassium as an electrolyte to replenish lost fluids in your body.

Food sources of potassium include avocado, mushrooms, meat, salmon, almonds, hemp seeds, and leafy greens, such as broccoli, brussels sprouts, and spinach.

There is no specific amount of potassium that you are required to include in your diet, but it is suggested that you have 3,500 mg each day to ensure that you don't develop a deficiency.

You can include a potassium supplement if you are not consuming enough potassium in your diet.

Magnesium

Magnesium is another nutrient that you should include in your diet to ensure proper bodily functions. Magnesium helps with DNA synthesis, improves the signals that travel from your nerves to your brain, and stabilizes your blood pressure and blood sugar levels.

Foods that are sources of magnesium include almonds, avocados, spinach, and tofu.

It is recommended that a woman over the age of 50 should have 320 mg of magnesium each day. You can also include a magnesium supplement into your diet if you have a magnesium deficiency. One of the signs of a magnesium deficiency that I have noticed is that you might experience muscle cramps. By taking a magnesium supplement, you can reduce this occurrence.

Iron

Iron is an essential nutrient that your body needs so that oxygenated blood can be transported around your body.

Food sources of iron include broccoli, spinach, tuna, shellfish, red meat, turkey, organ meats such as liver, kidneys, brain, heart, and tofu, and pumpkin seeds.

The amount of iron that you should have each day depends on various factors, such as your age, diet, genetics, and whether you are still menstruating or not.

A woman who is 50 years old should take 18 mg of iron each day. However, if you are 51 and older, you will decrease your intake to 7 mg each day.

Even if you do not have an iron deficiency, I recommend that you get an iron supplement. You can take it if you feel like you have no energy for the day or if you haven't gone through menopause yet and are nearing your cycle.

Omega-3 Fats

Omega-3 fats are an essential nutrient that your body needs to help maintain and protect brain function and eyesight and improve your immune system against illnesses such as ADHD, breast cancer, depression, and inflammatory diseases like arthritis.

Foods that contain omega-3 fats include anchovies, chia seeds, cod liver oil, flax seeds, herring, mackerel, oysters, salmon, sardines, and walnuts.

If you include fatty fish in your diet at least two times a week, you should be meeting your omega-3 dietary requirements. However, if you are not receiving enough omega-3 in your diet, then it is recommended that you take an omega-3 supplement.

Nutrients You Should Avoid at 50

Trans Fats

Fats that we receive from our diet can be grouped into three main categories: unsaturated fats, saturated fats, and trans fats. You can use unsaturated and saturated fats in the meals you eat and cook on the keto diet, but you should avoid using any trans fats.

Excess trans fats in your diet, such as baked goods, fried foods, hydrogenated vegetable oils, margarine, and ready-made meals, increase your "bad" low-density lipoprotein (LDL) and decrease your "good" high-density lipoprotein (HDL).

When you consume trans fats, your body cannot fully absorb these fats, and they accumulate in your blood and arteries. When this happens, your LDL cholesterol becomes elevated. LDL cholesterol can increase your blood pressure because your body has to work harder to pump blood through your body, and both of these factors can contribute to developing heart disease.

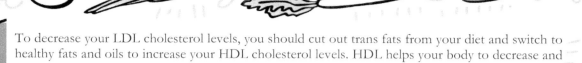

To decrease your LDL cholesterol levels, you should cut out trans fats from your diet and switch to healthy fats and oils to increase your HDL cholesterol levels. HDL helps your body to decrease and protect against LDL cholesterol.

Although you can use saturated fats such as butter, cheese, and heavy cream in your diet, it is suggested that you try to limit them, as they can also elevate your cholesterol levels. Whenever possible, try to replace saturated and trans fats with healthy unsaturated fats, including avocado, avocado oil, chia seeds, fatty fish, flax seeds, nuts, olive oil, and olives.

Added Sugars

Too much sugar in your diet increases triglyceride, which is the type of fat found in your bloodstream and tissues. Your body then uses these triglycerides to provide you with energy when you do not receive carbohydrates from foods—for example, between meals.

If your body cannot burn this energy, your triglyceride levels will be elevated, causing your blood pressure and blood sugar levels to increase. When you continue to expose your body to high triglycerides, you increase your risk of developing type 2 diabetes and heart disease.

When you choose to eat food containing lots of sugar, your daily calorie intake will be high. If you do not burn off the extra calories in your diet from sugar and are not active, you can gain weight. Excess weight can also be a contributing factor towards increased risk of type 2 diabetes and heart disease.

To avoid picking up any additional weight as you turn 50 and older, you should limit the added sugars you include in your diet and other food items with high sugar content. This includes chips, chocolate, desserts, pastries, soda, sweets, and food items with sugar and sweeteners added to them, such as sweetened dairy products.

Sodium

Sodium is an important nutrient to include in your diet. The average adult aged 50 and older should receive 1,200 to 1,300 mg of sodium in their diet each day at a minimum, but not more than 2,300 mg at most. The average American diet often sees people consuming as much as 3,400 mg of sodium each day, which can be bad for your health.

Many people experience low blood pressure, and they need to include more sodium in their diet, while others experience high blood pressure and are advised to decrease their sodium intake. You must find a balance between the minimum and maximum amounts that work for you and your diet to keep your sodium levels and blood pressure balanced throughout the day.

If you include too much sodium in your diet, you should check the nutritional information you are eating and how much sodium they contain. Ready-made meals and processed foods contain high levels of sodium. We also tend to add extra salt and spices to our meals when we do not need to. To decrease your sodium intake, you should choose food options that contain less sodium in them and look at cutting down on how much salt and extra spices you add to your dishes.

CHAPTER 3:

WHAT ARE THE BENEFITS OF A KETO DIET FOR WOMEN OVER 50?

When you turn 50 and older, you become more concerned with your health and the foods you are putting into your body. As you age, your metabolism slows down significantly, and you start to lose muscle mass, which causes you to gain weight. With the keto diet, you can improve your health and reduce your risk of developing heart disease, type 2 diabetes, and cancer.

Health Benefits

There are many other health benefits that you can receive from following a keto diet, including:

Reduce Your Appetite and Lose Weight

You can reduce your appetite and lose weight by eating a low-carb keto diet. In fact, in a recent meta-analysis published by the NIH (Mansoor et al., 2016), it was shown that you could lose up to 2 pounds more in a year by following the keto diet when compared to other diets. When you cut out carbohydrates and sugar from your diet and eat more fat and protein, you will find that you do not need to consume as many calories as you would on a non-keto diet and feel satiated longer.

Carbohydrates tend to make you feel bloated and heavy, and they only give your body energy for a short period, leaving you exhausted soon after eating them. Low-calorie foods are not only good for you to eat in your 50s to lose excess weight and reduce muscle loss, but they also help your body feel more energized and can reduce water retention and bloating.

Reduce the Risk of Heart Disease

Over 647,000 people die from heart disease in America each year. Various factors can cause heart disease, such as inflammation in the arteries of the heart, diabetes, cholesterol, high blood pressure, heart defects, smoking, stress, obesity, and not following a well-structured diet.

By eating healthy fats and oils from the keto diet, such as olive oil, you can increase your high-density lipoprotein (HDL) cholesterol and lower your low-density lipoprotein (LDL). HDL is a type of cholesterol that is good for your body and protects against LDL, the unhealthy cholesterol type. When you eat fats and oils that are bad for you, LDL increases in your bloodstream and can build up in your arteries' walls. When this happens, you can be at risk of heart disease. Healthy fats and oils help reduce LDL and improve your heart health, lowering your risk of developing heart disease.

High blood pressure, otherwise known as hypertension, is one of the main causes of heart disease. When you have high blood pressure, your heart needs to work harder to pump blood around your body, which can strain your heart. Because of this, your heart can become damaged, and it can progress into heart disease. A low-carb diet can help you normalize your blood pressure and lower your heart damage and heart disease risk.

A low-carb, high-fat diet like keto can help you lose excess weight, feel good about yourself, have lots of energy, and make healthier decisions about your body and nutrition. Weight loss, an exercise routine, and a structured eating plan that caters to your needs as your body ages will help you reduce your heart disease risk and improve your symptoms if you have developed heart disease.

Improve Type-2 Diabetes

Diabetes is a growing concern worldwide, with over 34 million people in the United States having diabetes. While a low-carb, high-fat diet like keto is not recommended for type 1 diabetics, it can be beneficial for those suffering from type 2 and lower their blood glucose levels. The keto diet can be the healthiest lifestyle change you can make to reduce your risk of developing type 2 diabetes and manage it effectively if you already suffer.

By reducing the number of calories that you consume each day in your diet, losing excess weight, and eating better food choices, you will be able to increase your body's sensitivity to insulin and reduce your blood sugar levels.

Many of the foods in the keto diet have a low glycemic load. This means that your blood sugar will not suddenly spike by eating these foods, compared to eating foods containing a high glycemic load. By eating foods with a low glycemic load, you can stabilize your blood sugar and reduce your body's need for insulin.

When you reduce your carbohydrates and increase your fat intake, your body creates ketones to process these facts into an energy source that your body can use throughout the day. Your body's process to create these ketones helps to improve your response and resistance to insulin.

Reduce the Risk of Cancer

The keto diet can help reduce your risk of developing cancer and is often used hand-in-hand with cancer treatment to improve your symptoms if you already have cancer.

It has been found that some tumors grow larger and can spread in the presence of glucose sugar. By restricting carbohydrates and sugar in your diet, you can reduce these cancerous growths and stop them from spreading further.

If you have cancer, you should talk to your general practitioner or nutritionist before starting the keto diet to get their advice and potentially monitor your cancerous cell growth while you are on the keto diet.

Improve Brain Disorders

The keto diet first came about as a diet to help treat children who have epilepsy and other brain disorders. Over the years, the keto diet for children was discovered, including those in their 50s or older.

When carbohydrates and sugars are removed from a person's diet, and their fat intake increases, their body cannot use either as an energy source. Their bodies and brains use ketones to burn the fat they consume from their diet to give them energy throughout the day. When this happens, the person's brain receives energy from the ketones produced in their body, and as a result, they experience fewer seizures. The keto diet can also benefit people who are suffering from Alzheimer's and Parkinson's disease. It has been shown that by eating a keto diet, you can decrease the symptoms associated with Alzheimer's disease and stop it from getting worse. Symptoms of Parkinson's disease can also be improved with the keto diet.

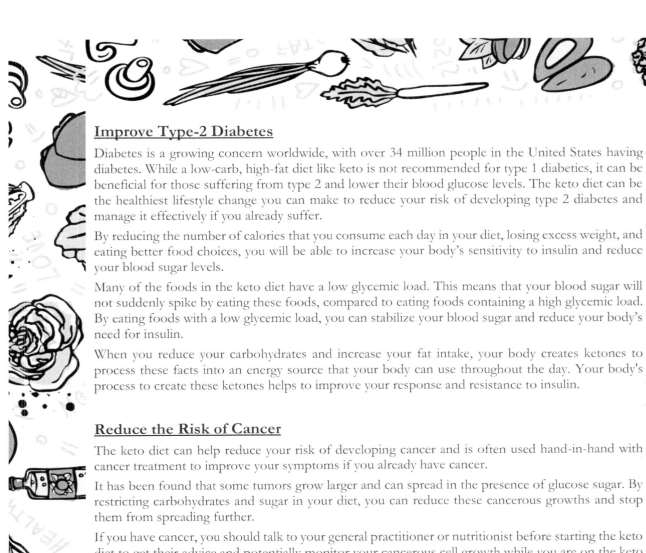

Improve Symptoms of PCOS

Polycystic ovary syndrome (PCOS) is a health condition whereby a woman's body produces more male hormones than it normally should. When this happens, you might experience irregular or skipped periods, and you will have problems getting pregnant. If you have PCOS, you have a higher risk of heart disease and developing type 2 diabetes.

When you eat foods that contain carbohydrates and sugar, your insulin levels increase. When your insulin levels are high, and you suffer from PCOS, your ovaries produce male hormones like testosterone, which in turn can cause your periods to become more irregular and cause you to grow more body hair.

By following a low-carb, high-fat keto diet, your insulin levels will remain steady and, as a result, your ovaries will not produce more male hormones in your body than it needs. This allows your period to become more regular and improves other PCOS symptoms that you might be experiencing.

Improve Symptoms of Metabolic Syndrome

When you are at risk of developing type 2 diabetes and heart disease, you will experience metabolic syndrome symptoms. This includes gaining weight around your stomach area. Your levels of "good" HDL cholesterol have decreased, and your "bad" LDL cholesterol has increased, high blood pressure, high blood sugar levels, and an increased number of triglycerides in your blood.

By following a low-carb, high fat keto diet, you will be able to treat and even reverse these symptoms and improve your quality of life by decreasing your risk of developing type 2 diabetes and heart disease. The keto diet can help you lose stomach weight, improve your "good" HDL cholesterol, stabilize your blood pressure and blood sugar levels, and decrease your blood's triglycerides.

Menopause

The keto diet can be beneficial to women at the age of 50 and older who are going through menopause. There are three phases of menopause that all women go through: perimenopause, menopause, and postmenopause. You are considered postmenopausal when you have not had a period in over 12 months.

Most women go through menopause in their late 40s to early 50s, but not all women experience it at the same age as other women, and you might find that you have gone through menopause early or that you are yet to go through menopause.

When you start, menopause will depend on various factors, such as when other women in your family like your mother, sister, or grandmother experienced menopause. Whether you use oral contraceptives or not, your weight, how many pregnancies you have had, whether you smoke or drink alcohol, and whether you are physically active or not.

Perimenopause is the phase you go through before you become menopausal and usually begins when you are in your mid to late 40s. When you go through perimenopause, your body will go through new changes.

You will start to experience various symptoms such as hot flashes, sleepless nights, feeling lethargic, vaginal dryness, breaking into hot sweats in the night, memory loss or struggling to focus, and having mood swings. These symptoms are worst in the perimenopause phase and continue into the menopause and postmenopausal stage. Many women who do not experience these symptoms severely in the perimenopausal stage might find that these symptoms worsen in the later menopausal and postmenopausal phases.

When a woman becomes perimenopausal, her estrogen and progesterone levels in her body decrease. Estrogen and progesterone are hormones used in a woman's body to help support the reproductive system's functioning and keep a woman's menstrual cycle regular. When these hormones decrease, your reproductive system will release fewer eggs, and your menstrual cycle will no longer be regular.

When you were younger, the estrogen hormone would work to distribute your stored fat into your hips and thighs. However, as you become older and your estrogen decreases, this fat is redirected to your stomach area. When fat stores in your stomach area, you become more at risk of developing heart disease, insulin resistance, and type 2 diabetes.

A decrease in estrogen levels, with an increase in the ghrelin hormone, triggers the feeling of hunger. You will find that your appetite and cravings will be increased, causing you to eat more food and gain weight at a faster rate than before you started menopause.

Other hormones that change during menopause and muscle loss that occurs as you turn 50 and older can also act against you during this time and make it easy to gain weight. A low-carb keto diet can help you manage your weight more effectively, decrease the amount of weight you gain, and help you get rid of food cravings.

With the reduction of estrogen in the body and removing energy sources like sugar and carbohydrates from your diet, your body and brain will create ketones that will use the fat you consume from the keto diet as an alternative energy source. Your hot flashes stem from receiving glucose in your brain, and when your brain no longer receives glucose from your diet, the severity and frequency of hot flashes that you experience are reduced. The keto diet has also been found to improve your mood and protect your memory against remembering things and improve your concentration.

It is suggested that when you follow the keto diet and go through menopause, you should further restrict your carbohydrate intake from the allowed 50 grams per day to between 20 to 30 grams per day so that your body goes into ketosis and can successfully help to relieve these symptoms.

CHAPTER 4

IMPORTANT TIPS FOR ACHIEVING SUCCESS WITH THE KETO DIET

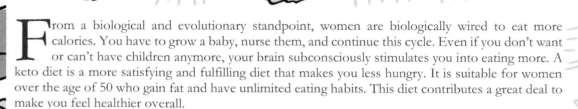

From a biological and evolutionary standpoint, women are biologically wired to eat more calories. You have to grow a baby, nurse them, and continue this cycle. Even if you don't want or can't have children anymore, your brain subconsciously stimulates you into eating more. A keto diet is a more satisfying and fulfilling diet that makes you less hungry. It is suitable for women over the age of 50 who gain fat and have unlimited eating habits. This diet contributes a great deal to make you feel healthier overall.

Here are some tips that will help you overcome pitfalls in this diet:

Eat more fat for the first few days and weeks

Women are more sensitive to calorie restriction and deficit. It is harder for women to be on a restricted diet than for men. Eating more fat will help you. There are numerous advantages to this strategy.

Firstly, it will give you motivation and boost up your morale. Many people are hesitant to eat fat, but you will eat it a lot and reduce weight in the process. Secondly, it will help you build fat reserves for future energy. Slowly, all your glycogen sources will melt, so it's better to replace them quickly. It can help your body adapt to using fats as a fuel source early on by boasting AMPK. Thirdly, you won't be working on an extreme calorie deficit. Your brain will signal that you have a sufficient amount of fat and a fuel source, which can induce a faster transition from glucose.

Don't try to restrict calories in the first weeks. The ketogenic diet is naturally calorie restricting. Simply cutting grains and sugar does half the job. For the first few weeks, don't stress yourself about precise calorie counting and excess carbs restriction. Eat from the allowed product list until you are full and eat again whenever you are hungry.

Undereating and overeating are not your concern right now. First, you have to go into ketosis and start getting used to not eating sugar and processed products.

Consider beginning with a fast

Metabolic depletion is not a good outcome. Even men who go through severe diet restrictions develop multiple problems. Calorie and diet restrictions put more burden on women than men, especially when they start.

Don't go overboard in the first few weeks and fast for a long time with keto dieting.

Both of them induce ketosis, and later on, it might be beneficial, but your body will become confused. It won't be able to decide whether harm or benefits are resulting from this scenario.

Aim for healthy fats

Direct fat consumption, or "fat bombs," is good for athletes because they already eat excessive fat amounts. These calories are later burned with intense workouts and sports. They can have direct spoonfuls of olive oil here and there, but not you. You need to combine different fats to get a healthy bowl rather than a nutritionally poor fat glass.

Some examples for a healthy quick fat bowl include soft boiled eggs with mustard and mayonnaise, avocado slices with sardines and green goddess dressing, low-carb vegetables filled with guacamole, etc.

Don't be too rigid

You need to plan and avoid being derailed, but this happens more often than you think. If your son comes to you with a surprise cookie he made, don't shunt him. This won't occur every day.

The reason for this diet may vary from person to person. However, after you have adapted to metabolizing fats, you will become tuned into burning more fat in general. You have already become metabolically resilient.

If you are an epileptic patient trying a keto diet to control seizures, enhance cancer drugs' effectiveness, or have other medical reasons for your diet, then be strict. Otherwise, you don't need to.

Don't follow diet trends

If you are in a scenario where you are not losing weight on this diet, the popular advice you will hear is to lower your carbs, lower your proteins, and lower your calories.

That's good advice but only for the people who have smoothly transitioned into this diet. People who experience this in the first couple of weeks are not intended for this advice. Normally, we all eat a high-carb diet, and suddenly switching it to keto will put some burden on your body. If you experience symptoms out of the ordinary or are generally really fatigued for a long time, it is better to consume some protein and carbs. Lowering something doesn't always provide good results.

Don't skimp on protein

One of the suggestions you will hear when you are not losing weight on this diet or are having various symptoms is to drop protein. Carbs need to be low, and fats need to be high, but where does protein go? It depends on what kind of keto diet you are following, but you should never drop protein, whatever kind you are.

No matter if you are starting or have been dieting for a long time, this should be ingrained in your mind. If you want to lose muscle mass, energy, and strength, there is no use for this diet.

Your diet makes you healthier and gets you in better shape—not to starve yourself and force your body to eat itself.

CHAPTER 5:

WHY IS A NORMAL KETO DIET NOT RECOMMENDED FOR WOMEN OVER 50?

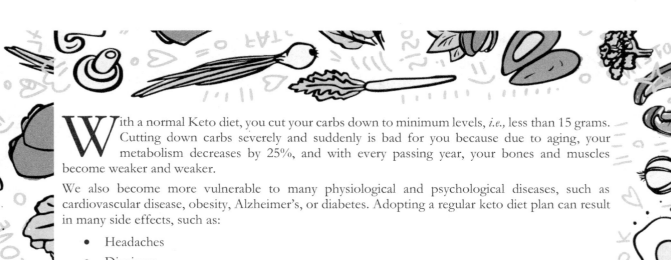

With a normal Keto diet, you cut your carbs down to minimum levels, *i.e.,* less than 15 grams. Cutting down carbs severely and suddenly is bad for you because due to aging, your metabolism decreases by 25%, and with every passing year, your bones and muscles become weaker and weaker.

We also become more vulnerable to many physiological and psychological diseases, such as cardiovascular disease, obesity, Alzheimer's, or diabetes. Adopting a regular keto diet plan can result in many side effects, such as:

- Headaches
- Dizziness
- Fatigue
- Brain fog and difficulty focusing
- Lack of motivation and irritability
- Nausea
- Keto flu
- Inflammation

These side effects cause many women to pull back and lose hope. It's all because you haven't been told before about the likely side effects you can suffer if you dive headfirst into the Keto diet.

For this, you need a specific Keto diet plan, which will benefit you via weight loss, help build muscles, stabilize your blood sugar levels, and maximize your energy levels. And for all this, the Keto diet for women over 50 is a perfect option for you.

This diet's health benefits are not different for men or women, but the speed at which goals are reached does differ. As mentioned, women's bodies are a lot different when it comes to burning fats and losing weight. For example, by design, women have at least 10% more body fat than men. It doesn't matter how fit you are; this is just an aspect of being a woman you must consider. Don't be hard on yourself if you notice that it seems like men can lose weight easier — that's because they can! What women have in additional body fat, men typically have in muscle mass. This is why men tend to see faster external results because that added muscle mass means that their metabolism rates are higher. That increased metabolism means that fat and energy get burned faster. When you are on keto, though, the internal change is happening right away.

Your metabolism is unique, but it will also be slower than a man's metabolism by nature. Since muscle can burn more calories than fat, the weight just seems to fall off men, giving them the ability to reach the opportunity for muscle growth quickly. This should not be something that holds you back from starting your keto journey. As long as you keep realistic bodily factors in mind, you won't be left wondering why it takes you a little longer to start losing weight.

Another unique condition that a woman can experience but a man cannot is Polycystic Ovary Syndrome (PCOS), a hormonal imbalance that causes cysts' development. These cysts can cause pain, interfere with normal reproductive function, and burst in extreme and dangerous cases. PCOS is very common among women, affecting up to 10% of the entire female population. Surprisingly, most

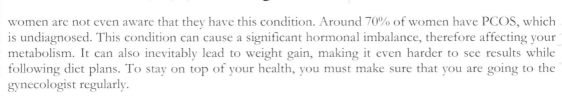

women are not even aware that they have this condition. Around 70% of women have PCOS, which is undiagnosed. This condition can cause a significant hormonal imbalance, therefore affecting your metabolism. It can also inevitably lead to weight gain, making it even harder to see results while following diet plans. To stay on top of your health, you must make sure that you are going to the gynecologist regularly.

Menopause is another reality that must be faced by women, especially as we age. The majority of women begin the process of menopause in their mid-40s. Men do not go through menopause, so they are spared from another condition that causes slower metabolism and weight gain. When you start menopause, it is easy to gain weight and lose muscle. Once menopause begins, most women lose muscle faster, and conversely, gain weight despite dieting and exercise regimens. Keto can, therefore, be the right diet plan for you. Regardless of what your body is doing naturally through processes like menopause, your internal systems will be making the switch from running on carbs to deriving energy from fats.

Because the keto diet reduces the amount of sugar you are consuming, it naturally lowers insulin in your bloodstream. This can have amazing effects on any existing PCOS and fertility issues and menopausal symptoms and conditions like pre-diabetes and type 2 diabetes. Once your body adjusts to the keto diet, you are overcoming the naturally occurring things, preventing you from losing weight and getting healthy. Even if you placed your body on a strict diet, if it isn't getting rid of sugars properly, you likely aren't going to see the same results you will when you try going keto. This is a big reason why keto diets can be so beneficial for women.

As we've deliberated, carbs and sugar can have a huge impact on your hormonal balance. You might not even realize that your hormones are not in balance until you experience a lifestyle that limits carbs and eliminates sugars. Keto is going to reset this balance for you, keeping your hormones at healthy levels. As a result of this, you'll find that you will feel better, healthier, and younger by implementing the simple steps that will tune your body into processing excess fats for energy. You'll build muscle, lose fat, and feel much more energy to get through your days.

Bodily Changes After 50

Many people attribute aging to sickness and pains, but this assumption doesn't have to be. Getting old doesn't mean a decline in good health. However, it comes with some levels of decline in the body's systematic function when you begin to age. This decline in bodily functions doesn't have to be painful and isolating.

The sad reality is that many seniors don't have the proper diet guide to balance their bodies and keep them functioning optimally at old age. Furthermore, many seniors without a proper diet often engage in the consumption of high-carb diets, which is neither healthy nor helpful for people aged 50 and above.

With a proper keto diet plan, old age isn't as unfortunate as many see it. A good diet plan will help your physical and mental health as you age.

CHAPTER 6:

WHAT YOU EAT DAILY ON
THE KETO DIET

These foods can give you control over your post-menopausal symptoms in addition to being a good, low carb, keto-friendly snack.

Flaxseed

It has been found that flaxseed helps with lowering the severity of hot flashes and other menopausal symptoms. However, more research needs to be done before any conclusive statements can be made.

Green Tea

Green tea is extremely healthy because of its high supply of antioxidants. One of the antioxidants present in this tea is catechins; they have been shown to stabilize metabolism and increase heart health.

Caffeinated green tea decreases the amount of insulin in menopausal women, whereas decaffeinated green tea doesn't provide the same result. If you have high levels of insulin, you can give green tea a try.

Fatty Fish

This is a good source of healthy omega-3s, such as DHA and EPA. Its consumption has been linked to reduced insulin resistance, inflammation, and triglycerides (or bad fat).

They also show these results in menopausal women. A study done on post-menopausal women revealed a dose of omega-3s decreased insulin resistance, blood pressure, and inflammatory markers.

Lifestyle Changes

Some changes are required when you enter this stage of your life. You need to be extra vigilant and care more about your body and mental health.

Regular Exercise

There is no question that exercise leads to a better quality of life, regardless of age or gender. Studies have shown that menopausal women who regularly exercise experience less stress, less muscle loss, and an increase in fat metabolism.

Although all exercises are great and show positive results, strength training is the most effective for post-menopausal women. An example of strength training is lifting weights.

Yoga

Yoga has been shown to relieve stress in randomized studies. However, there has been less research on the topic of menopausal women. One study found that yoga and other mind-body therapies help

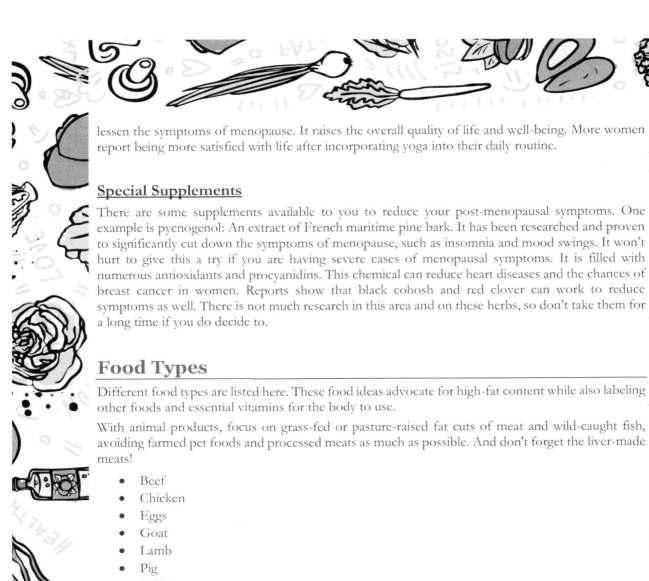

lessen the symptoms of menopause. It raises the overall quality of life and well-being. More women report being more satisfied with life after incorporating yoga into their daily routine.

Special Supplements

There are some supplements available to you to reduce your post-menopausal symptoms. One example is pycnogenol: An extract of French maritime pine bark. It has been researched and proven to significantly cut down the symptoms of menopause, such as insomnia and mood swings. It won't hurt to give this a try if you are having severe cases of menopausal symptoms. It is filled with numerous antioxidants and procyanidins. This chemical can reduce heart diseases and the chances of breast cancer in women. Reports show that black cohosh and red clover can work to reduce symptoms as well. There is not much research in this area and on these herbs, so don't take them for a long time if you do decide to.

Food Types

Different food types are listed here. These food ideas advocate for high-fat content while also labeling other foods and essential vitamins for the body to use.

With animal products, focus on grass-fed or pasture-raised fat cuts of meat and wild-caught fish, avoiding farmed pet foods and processed meats as much as possible. And don't forget the liver-made meats!

- Beef
- Chicken
- Eggs
- Goat
- Lamb
- Pig
- Rabbit
- Turkey
- Venison
- Shellfish
- Chicken
- Cow
- Goat
- Lamb
- Pork
- Salmon
- Tuna
- Halibut
- Cod

- Gelatin
- Chicken fat
- Coconut fat
- Duck fat
- Ghee
- Lard
- Tallow
- MCT oil
- Avocado oil
- Macadamia oil
- Extra virgin olive oil
- Coconut butter
- Coconut

Instead of root vegetables and other starchy veggies, you need to be vigilant about carbohydrates in the ketogenic diet, so stick to leafy greens and low-glycemic veggies. I've put avocados in this section because some of us may think it is a vegetable even though it's a fruit.

- Artichokes
- Asparagus
- Avocado
- Broccoli
- Bell peppers
- Cauliflower
- Cabbage
- Celery
- Cucumber
- Lettuce
- Kohlrabi
- Radishes
- Zucchini
- Okra or ladies ' fingers
- Seaweed
- Tomatoes
- Spinach
- Watercress

If you can handle dairy products, you can add full-fat, raw dairy products in your diet and unpasteurized. Keep in mind that some brands contain lots of sugar that could increase the carb content, so look out for nutrition labels and limit these items' intake. When possible, go for the full-fat varieties as they are less likely to substitute the fat with sugar.

- Cottage cheese
- Mozzarella cheese
- Swiss cheese
- Sour cream
- Full-fat yogurt
- Heavy cream

Herbs and spices are an excellent way to flavor your foods while adding a moderate number of calories or carbs.

- Black pepper
- Basil
- Cinnamon
- Cayenne
- Cilantro
- Chili powder
- Cumin
- Curry powder
- Garam masala
- Ginger
- Nutmeg
- Garlic
- Oregano
- Onion
- Paprika
- Parsley
- Rosemary
- Sea salt
- Sage
- Thyme
- Turmeric
- White pepper

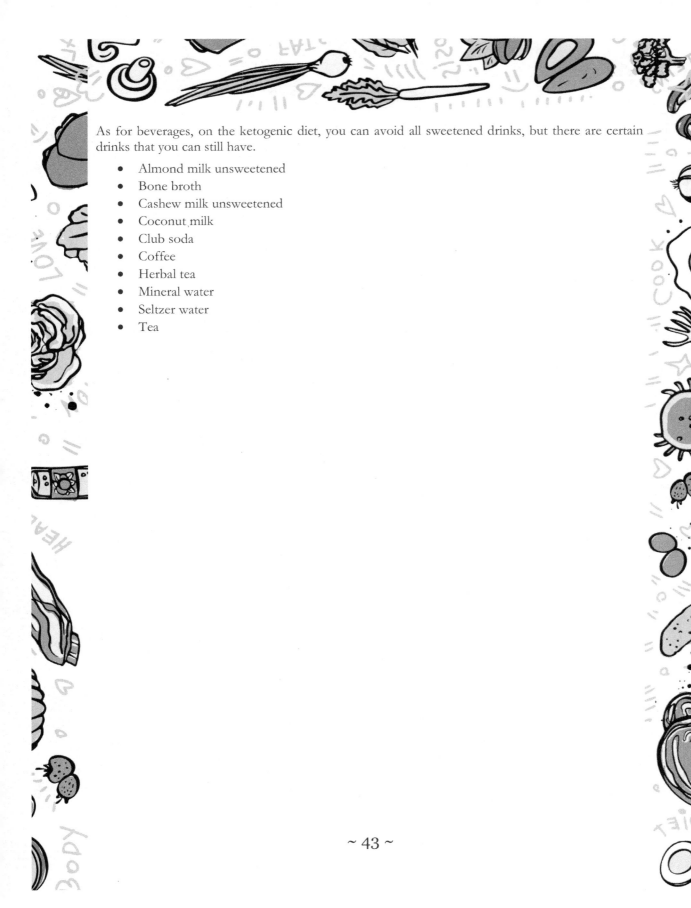

As for beverages, on the ketogenic diet, you can avoid all sweetened drinks, but there are certain drinks that you can still have.

- Almond milk unsweetened
- Bone broth
- Cashew milk unsweetened
- Coconut milk
- Club soda
- Coffee
- Herbal tea
- Mineral water
- Seltzer water
- Tea

CHAPTER 7:

FOODS TO AVOID ON
THE KETO DIET FOR WOMEN OVER 50

We now need to talk about the foods you can't have on a keto diet. This list is a good summary, but it is not exhaustive, so be sure to do research into anything you're adding to your diet that is not covered in this chapter.

Soda

What, no soda? You've got to be kidding me! Sorry, folks, I like a good fountain drink of soda just like the next person, but I'm afraid it's all too true. If you want to engage in intermittent fasting, you will have to leave your soda behind. This is not meant as a punishment—it's simply the reality of the beast. One of the major components of an intermittent fast, after all, is the avoidance of sugar. It's so your body will start burning fat stores already in place that we refrain from guzzling sugary soda for our metabolic rate to nibble on during fasting. So yes, for the time being, as you engage in an intermittent fasting routine, you will indeed have to forego soda.

Heavily Processed Food

As you have probably already picked up on during this book, processed foods are frowned upon. Anything that has been processed and packaged will have a ton of preservatives packed into them, which will have a long-term effect on your system over time while generally harmless. Heavily processed food will also pose a direct interference with your metabolism. That's why the fresher the food, the better when it comes to intermittent fasting.

Sugary Sweets

Just like with sugary sodas, sugary sweets would be completely counterproductive for an intermittent fast. The goal of an intermittent fast, after all, is to switch the body from burning sugar and carbs to burning our latent fat deposits instead. Eating sugary sweets would disrupt this process and add more junk to the fat already deposited in our trunks. So yes, you must avoid sugary sweets at all costs while you participate in intermittent fasting.

Alcohol

I don't mean to be a party pooper or anything but let me just go ahead and say it. Alcohol and intermittent fasting do not mix. The reason? Alcohol has a direct effect on fat-burning metabolism. And the last thing you would want to do is wreck your fast by throwing a wrench in your fat-burning metabolism! Alcohol also carries carbs, sugars, calories, and the like. So, yeah, just like drinking and driving—drinking and fasting should be avoided.

Refined Grains

Unlike whole grains, refined grains will indeed have a decidedly negative impact on your fast. Refined grains, once metabolized, will turn directly into sugar. As already mentioned a few times in this chapter, sugar will defeat the purpose of your fast.

The whole purpose of intermittent fasting is to get your body to stop burning sugar as fuel and burn fat instead. Ingesting refined grains that turn into sugar, therefore, completely negates this process. It will also raise your insulin levels. Having that said, refined grains are to be avoided if at all possible.

Trans-Fats

Trans-fats are just bad to perfectly shape the body. No good can come from them. And most especially, no good could come from your fast by ingesting them. Trans-fat, the fatty acids found in certain milk and meat products should be avoided while you participate in an intermittent fast. It raises cholesterol, insulin, and wrecks any chance you may have had a successful fast. Just say no, when it comes to trans-fat.

Fast Food

Even though we call it "fast food,"—the burgers and fries we bag from places like McDonald's are not exactly the best thing to eat during an intermittent fast! One look at an overly processed, carb-dense meal from McDonald's, and I think you might probably understand why.

At any rate, presented here are the foods that you should and shouldn't eat. Take note and take heart. Enjoy your fast!

CHAPTER 8:

MOST COMMON MISTAKES AND HOW TO AVOID THEM

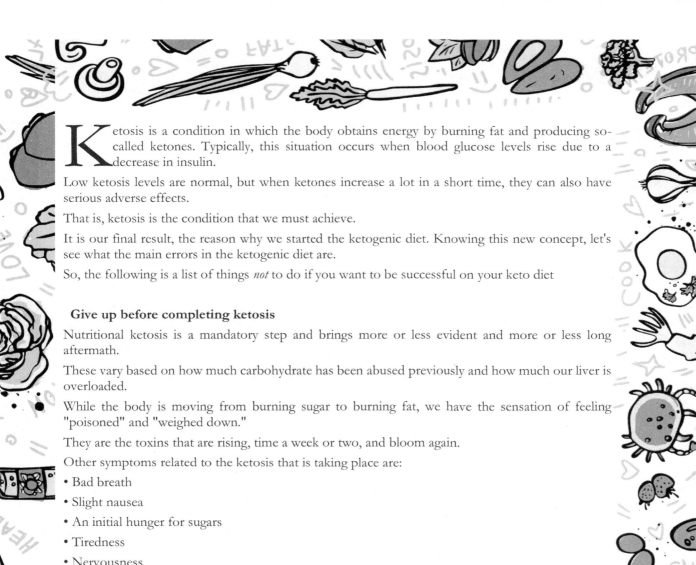

Ketosis is a condition in which the body obtains energy by burning fat and producing so-called ketones. Typically, this situation occurs when blood glucose levels rise due to a decrease in insulin.

Low ketosis levels are normal, but when ketones increase a lot in a short time, they can also have serious adverse effects.

That is, ketosis is the condition that we must achieve.

It is our final result, the reason why we started the ketogenic diet. Knowing this new concept, let's see what the main errors in the ketogenic diet are.

So, the following is a list of things *not* to do if you want to be successful on your keto diet

Give up before completing ketosis

Nutritional ketosis is a mandatory step and brings more or less evident and more or less long aftermath.

These vary based on how much carbohydrate has been abused previously and how much our liver is overloaded.

While the body is moving from burning sugar to burning fat, we have the sensation of feeling "poisoned" and "weighed down."

They are the toxins that are rising, time a week or two, and bloom again.

Other symptoms related to the ketosis that is taking place are:

• Bad breath

• Slight nausea

• An initial hunger for sugars

• Tiredness

• Nervousness

• A slight sadness

These latter symptoms are linked to the impact that the elimination of sugars and carbohydrates has on our minds, which, by stimulating the same opiate receptors, makes us feel happy and satisfied.

Now by stopping them and losing this stimulus, it may happen that, on the contrary, we feel a little sad and nervous.

Many are frightened of these symptoms and not being well informed. They believe that the ketogenic diet is not for them, that they are worse than when they started and abandon everything before going all the way to ketosis.

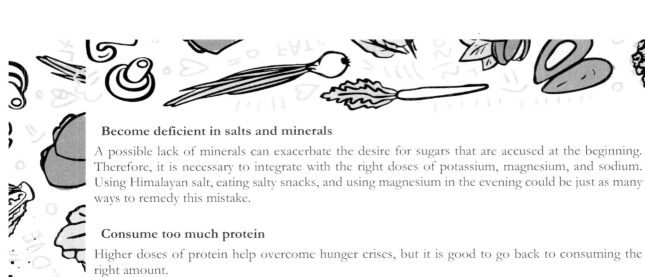

Become deficient in salts and minerals

A possible lack of minerals can exacerbate the desire for sugars that are accused at the beginning. Therefore, it is necessary to integrate with the right doses of potassium, magnesium, and sodium. Using Himalayan salt, eating salty snacks, and using magnesium in the evening could be just as many ways to remedy this mistake.

Consume too much protein

Higher doses of protein help overcome hunger crises, but it is good to go back to consuming the right amount.

To find out how many proteins to consume, just multiply your body weight by 0.8 (if you exercise regularly) or 1.2 (if you are an athlete).

Another common mistake is to consume poor-quality proteins, such as pork and cold cuts.

Insufficient fat consumption

This is another mistake that is easy to run into if we follow the ketogenic diet. We continue to be afraid of consuming fats and not using all-natural sources: coconut oil, ghee, MCT oil, egg yolk, fatty fish, and butter, avocado. The opposite mistake is to exaggerate with oilseeds: walnuts, almonds, flax seeds, pumpkin seeds. If we neglect to soak in advance with water and lemon, we also absorb the physic acid they contain, a pro substance inflammatory and antinutrient.

Consume bad quality food

It is another of the most common mistakes. We focus on weight loss but continue to consume frozen, canned, highly processed food and, as mentioned, proteins that are practical and quick to eat but of low quality.

Do not introduce the right amount of fiber

Vegetables should always be fresh, consumed in twice the amount of protein, and always cooked intelligently, never subjected to overcooking or too high temperatures.

In everyday life, if present, however, we often resort to ready-made, frozen, or packaged vegetables.

Also, concerning fruit, we often resort to the very sugary one; we forget that there are many berries with a low glycemic index: berries, mulberries, goji berries, Inca berries, maqui.

Eat raw vegetables

I know this may surprise you, but consuming large quantities of raw vegetables, centrifuged, cold smoothies, over time slow down digestion, cool it, undermine our ability to transform food and absorb nutrients. Over time, this exposes us to inevitable deficiencies: joint pain, teeth, nails and weak hair, anemia, tiredness, abnormal weight loss.

Consume the highest protein load at dinner

It is a mistake that, involuntarily, we all commit. The work, the thousand commitments, leads us to stay out all day, to eat a frugal meal for lunch, or even not to consume it at all. Here dinner turns into the only moment of the day which we spend with our family members. We have more time, we are more relaxed, and we finally allow ourselves a real meal complete with vegetables, proteins, sometimes even carbohydrates, and then fruit or dessert to finish.

It escapes us that even for the healthiest protein, the freshest or most organic food weighs down the liver. During the night, this being busy helping digestion, it cannot perform the other precious task: to purify the blood, prepare hormones, and energize for the next day.

Not drinking enough

And above all, don't drink hot water. You got it right. Drinking hot water is another story entirely, a massive difference from drinking it even at room temperature. The benefits are many: more excellent digestibility and absorption, deep hydration of cells, brighter skin and hair, retention disappear, cellulite improves, kidneys are strengthened, digestion improves, heartburn subsides.

So, in conclusion, if you avoid these nine mistakes:

- give up before completing ketosis
- incurring deficiencies in salts and minerals
- consuming too much protein

- consume few fats
- consume lousy quality food
- do not introduce the right amount of fiber

- consume raw vegetables
- introduce the highest protein load in the evening
- do not drink incredibly hot water

That is, to allow the body to enter and exit the state of ketosis, use fats as energy fuel, and burn glucose when we have it available.

CHAPTER 9:

ENTERING KETOSIS

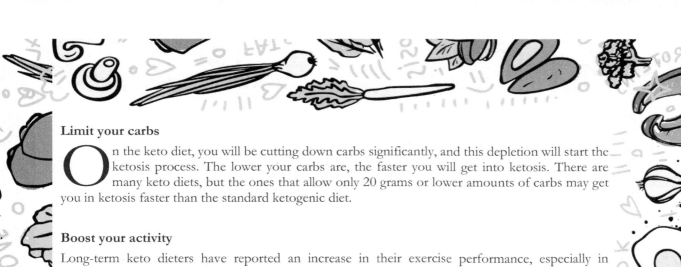

Limit your carbs

On the keto diet, you will be cutting down carbs significantly, and this depletion will start the ketosis process. The lower your carbs are, the faster you will get into ketosis. There are many keto diets, but the ones that allow only 20 grams or lower amounts of carbs may get you in ketosis faster than the standard ketogenic diet.

Boost your activity

Long-term keto dieters have reported an increase in their exercise performance, especially in endurance exercises. However, studies also show that exercise drastically increases the level of ketone bodies in your blood.

One small study took a few older women and tested their ketone levels after exercise before and after meals. The ketones were approximately 200% higher when they exercised before meals.

Before exercising, it is better to have a lower or less demanding exercise routine in the first weeks of the diet. During this time, your body is in a transitional period, and your exercise performance will decrease at this time.

Increase your intake of MCTs

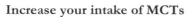

Not all fats are the same. MCTs are medium-chain triglycerides. They get absorbed by the liver way faster than other forms of fat and quickly supply the ketone bodies your body needs for energy.

Studies have found that consuming high amounts of MCTs can induce ketosis without the need for extreme carbohydrate restrictions. If they are added to your diet, you can reach ketosis more quickly.

There are many kinds of MCTs, but one of the most important ones for getting you into ketosis is lauric acid. They are metabolized gradually and, therefore, helps in sustaining ketosis as well. They are more often found in coconut oil.

There are two ways you can get MCTs—either from natural sources like coconut oil, flaxseed oil, or olive oil, or you can get a higher concentrated dose from MCT supplement oils. They can be added to smoothies, used as dressings, and topped over your meals.

Eat a lot of healthy fats

When you are following this diet, you will consume plenty of fatty ingredients. This will boost your ketone levels and get you into ketosis early. The goal is not to increase your fat uptake but increase the quality of fat.

In this diet, fats are to be consumed, but the important thing is to have diverse sources, including lots of healthy fats. Don't just stick to coconut oil for MCTs; eat fish and avocados as well. Each ingredient will bring something new to your plate.

However, if your goal is weight loss, you need to be extra careful about not eating too many calories. Eating too much fat may stop you from losing weight if you are not careful about your calories.

Consider fasting

Several studies show fasting as a highly effective way to get into ketosis. Some of us go into a mild state of ketosis before breakfast. That is because our bodies have gone 8–10 hours without eating, and it starts to break out fat reserves for energy. Children who have epilepsy usually fast for half a day before starting a keto diet to enter ketosis quickly and stop their seizures.

Intermittent fasting is also a great way to induce ketosis quickly. A new form of fasting, called fat fasting, is being investigated. With this, individuals have to take 90% of calories from fat. Some studies have shown this to be effective, but there needs to be more experiments.

Have a good protein intake

Your protein intake shouldn't be low or very high on this diet. If you don't have a proper ratio of protein, this can lead to detrimental effects.

Firstly, you are already low on carbs. It decreases the glycogen in your muscles. If you don't have protein either, the muscles will start to eat their protein for energy, and muscle mass will shrink. You will become weaker. If you have proper proteins, then muscle loss can be avoided.

Secondly, protein is needed for various functions—building enzymes and hormones and processes like gluconeogenesis. This process makes glucose from non-carbohydrate sources to supply energy to cells that can only use glucose, like red blood cells.

Test ketone levels and adjust accordingly

Everyone reacts to diets differently, and you have to make customized changes to your diet according to your ketone levels. You text ketones in three ways: blood, breath, and urine. The accuracy and cost of goods are highest for blood and lowest for urine.

Once you have decided on how you will track ketone levels, try adjustments, and see whether they are effective or not. Keep the ones that yield positive results while discarding others.

CHAPTER 10:

SIGNS THAT YOU ARE IN KETOSIS

Since the human body heavily depends on carbs, it always takes time to adapt according to the new ketogenic lifestyle. It's like changing the fuel of a machine when the body is switched to the ketogenic diet; it shows some different signs than usual, which are as follows:

1. Increased Urination
Ketones are normally known as a diuretic, which means that they help remove the extra water out of the body through increased urination. So high levels of ketones mean more urination than normal. Due to ketosis, more acetoacetate is released about three times faster than the usual, which is excreted along with urine, and its release then causes more urination.

2. Dry Mouth
It is obvious that more urination means the loss of high amounts of water, which causes dehydration as more water is released out of the body due to ketosis. Along with those fluids, many metabolites and electrolytes are also excreted out of the body. Therefore, it is always recommended that you increase water consumption on a ketogenic diet and have a good intake of electrolytes to maintain the body's water levels. It helps to incorporate more salty things (like pickles) into your meals.

3. Bad Breath
A ketone, which is known as acetone, is released through our breath. This ketone has a distinct smell, and it takes some time to go away. Due to ketosis, many acetones are released through the breath, which causes bad breath. It can be reduced with the help of a fresh mouth.

4. Reduced Appetite and Lasting Energy
It is the clearest sign of ketosis. Since fat molecules are high-energy macronutrients, each molecule is broken down to produce three times more energy than a carb molecule. Therefore, a person feels more energized round the clock.

CHAPTER 11:

INTERMITTENT FASTING AND
A KETOGENIC DIET

Much like the ketogenic diet, intermittent fasting is picking up more popularity by the year!. If it is an eating pattern, you will follow with periods of fasting and periods of eating. When you eat in this manner, you will be focusing on the foods allowed on the ketogenic diet and deciding when you are going to eat them.

Fasting has been practiced throughout our entire time on earth. When you think about it, our ancestors did not have food available year-round. When they could not find food, they had to learn how to function without food for extended periods. In the modern world, we have a McDonald's at every corner, both a blessing and a curse! For this reason, fasting is much more natural for us compared to eating three or even four meals in a day!

Fasting Methods

If this is your first time trying the ketogenic diet, you may want to wait to incorporate this eating style. It will be enough work figuring out what you are allowed to eat on the ketogenic diet. When you are ready, there are several types of intermittent fasting that you can try out. Much like with our diets, everyone is allowed to be on a different schedule. What works for you may not work for your friend! But this is one of the best parts of the diet; it is completely customizable to your needs!

16/8 Method

This first popular method is known as the Leangains Protocol. For this method, you will skip breakfast and only eat for eight hours during the day. An example of this could be 12-8p.m. Once those hours are up, you would then fast for sixteen hours. During your fast, you eat nothing or very little amounts of food if you are desperate.

5:2 Diet

This next method is a bit different compared to typical fasting. For the 5:2 diet, you spend two days eating only 500-600 calories. On the rest of the days, you are allowed to eat normally.

Eat-Stop-Eat

The Eat-Stop-Eat fasting method involves not eating for 24 hours straight for one or two days a week. On the other days, you are allowed to eat normally.

Crescendo Method

For women over 50, this may be your best option. For the crescendo method, you will only be fasting for 12-16 hours for 2-3 days a week. These days of fasting should be nonconsecutive and spaced throughout your week. For example, you would want to fast for Monday, Wednesday, and again on Friday.

Intermittent fasting works because, during these fasts, you are reducing your overall calorie intake for the week. The fewer calories you consume, the more weight you are going to lose

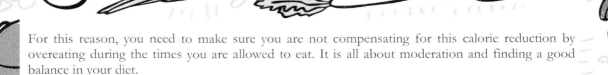

For this reason, you need to make sure you are not compensating for this calorie reduction by overeating during the times you are allowed to eat. It is all about moderation and finding a good balance in your diet.

Intermittent Fasting and Hormones

As you follow the Ketogenic Diet combined with intermittent fasting, several things will be happening to you on a molecular and cellular level. One of the major benefits is that your body will adjust your hormone levels to make your body fat more accessible as you fast. It is beneficial on the Ketogenic Diet because you are now using the fat as energy, anyway!

Fasting also initiates cellular repair within your body. This process is known as autophagy. During autophagy, your cells begin to digest and remove any dysfunctional proteins that are old and built up inside of your cells. Fasting also helps promote proper gene expression that may help protect against disease and help you live a longer and healthier life!

Intermittent Fasting and Weight Loss

If you are looking to lose weight on the Ketogenic Diet, it will be beneficial to pair it with Intermittent Fasting. With this eating, you will be eating fewer meals and automatically reducing your number of calories. Once this is complete, your body will begin lowering the insulin in your system and increasing the number of fat-burning hormones in your system. It means that you can increase your metabolic rate and get rid of that excess weight through short-term fasting!

Health Benefits of Intermittent Fasting

While weight loss is an incredible benefit in itself, Intermittent Fasting will offer you several other benefits as well. Some of the other benefits include:

• Decreased Inflammation

• Improved Heart Health

• Increased Brain Health

• Increased Life Spans

Intermittent Fasting can also help lead you to a simpler lifestyle. When you are eating three to four meals a day, this requires a lot of time to cook and plan healthy meals. When you are only eating for a certain amount of time, this gives you more time to do what you want without worrying about fitting a meal in!

Risks of Intermittent Fasting

With those benefits in mind, it should be stated that Intermittent Fasting is not for everyone. For example, if you are underweight or have a history of eating disorders, you will want to consult with a professional before beginning intermittent fasting or the ketogenic diet. With these two methods combined, your diet will be doing you more harm than good.

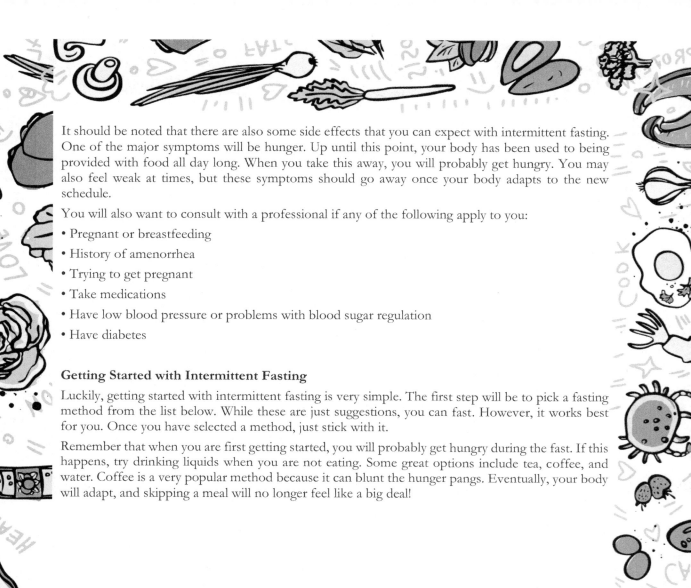

It should be noted that there are also some side effects that you can expect with intermittent fasting. One of the major symptoms will be hunger. Up until this point, your body has been used to being provided with food all day long. When you take this away, you will probably get hungry. You may also feel weak at times, but these symptoms should go away once your body adapts to the new schedule.

You will also want to consult with a professional if any of the following apply to you:

• Pregnant or breastfeeding

• History of amenorrhea

• Trying to get pregnant

• Take medications

• Have low blood pressure or problems with blood sugar regulation

• Have diabetes

Getting Started with Intermittent Fasting

Luckily, getting started with intermittent fasting is very simple. The first step will be to pick a fasting method from the list below. While these are just suggestions, you can fast. However, it works best for you. Once you have selected a method, just stick with it.

Remember that when you are first getting started, you will probably get hungry during the fast. If this happens, try drinking liquids when you are not eating. Some great options include tea, coffee, and water. Coffee is a very popular method because it can blunt the hunger pangs. Eventually, your body will adapt, and skipping a meal will no longer feel like a big deal!

CHAPTER 12:

LOW COST, EASY TO FOLLOW, AND EFFECTIVE MONTHLY KETO MEAL PLAN FOR FAT LOSS

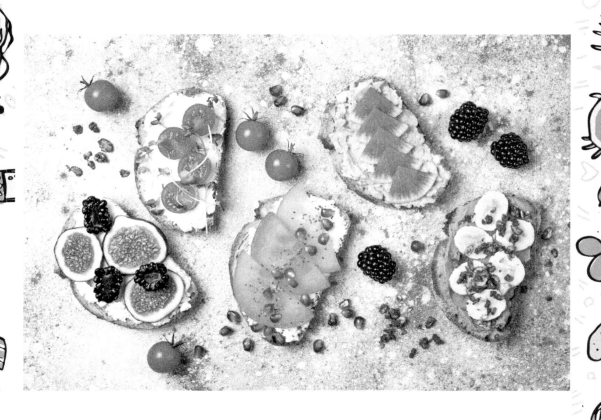

30 DAY MEAL PLAN

Week 1

- Each day will be between 1,500-1,700 calories (designed for weight loss).
- Be flexible! Feel free to replace any of the recipes or ingredients with your personal choices and adjust the ingredient amounts to fit your macros and situation.
- If you follow a very strict keto diet, make sure to personalize this meal plan (to make it work for you.

Meal Plan

Week 1	Breakfast	Lunch	Dinner
Monday	Low-Carb Gluten-Free Pancakes	Beef Burgers	Beef-Stuffed Mushrooms
Tuesday	Pan-Fried Mushrooms, Boiled Eggs, Spinach and Capsicum	Delicious Keto Potato Wedges	Garlic Parmesan Chicken Wings
Wednesday	Ground Beef, Eggs and Avocado Breakfast Bowl	Stuffed Zucchini	Chicken Pesto
Thursday	Chicken and Vegetable Breakfast Casserole	Keto Veggie Dish	Sesame-Crusted Tuna with Green Beans
Friday	Savory Broccoli Muffins	Broccoli and Turkey Dish	Beef Stir Fry
Saturday	Egg Salmon Breakfast Bake	Keto Cheese Potato	Slow Cooker Pot Roast with Green Beans
Sunday	Avocado and Egg Breakfast	Easy Bacon Jalapeno Wings	Grilled Pork with Salsa

Shopping List

PANTRY

(Check your pantry before shopping as you may already have some of these items)

Salt (1 Box, If Needed)

Pepper (1 Box, If Needed)

White Pepper (1/8 Tsp.)

Cinnamon (¼ Tsp.)

Mustard Vinaigrette (4.4g)

Curry Powder (1 Tbsp)

Whole Wheat Flour (4 Oz)

Paprika (1/4 Tsp)

FRESH PRODUCE

Yellow Onion (2 Medium)

Garlic (1 Peg)

Spinach (2 cups)

Roma Tomato (3)

Kalamata Olives (8 Pieces)

Fresh Parsley (1.5 bunch)

Red Beets (8.8 Oz, Large)

Yellow Beets (8.8 Oz, Small)

Mesclun (4.3 Oz.)

Grilled Vegetable Medley (1 Pack)

Lemon (1)

Blueberries (0.3 oz)

Broccoli (3 oz, florets)

Zucchini

Avocadoes

PROTEIN

Eggs (4, large)

Chicken breast (4 (24 oz), boneless, skinless)

Ground beef

Tuna
Pork
Pot roast
Salmon

DAIRY

Skim milk (3L)

feta cheese (15 tbsp, crumbled)

Ricotta cheese (2.1 oz)

GRAINS, NUTS, SEEDS, AND LEGUMES

(Check your pantry before shopping as you may already have some of these items)

Oats (2 ½ cup, raw)

Assorted nuts, blanched and slivered (0.3 oz)

Walnuts (0.1 oz)

Whole Wheat Bread (1 loaf)

Brown Rice (1 cup)

DRIED/DEHYDRATED FRUITS

Peach (1, chopped)

Raisins (2 cups)

Dried cranberries (2½ cup)

HERBS

(Check your pantry before shopping as you may already have some of these items)

Dried thyme (1 container, if needed -1/8 tsp needed for recipe)

Coriander (1/2 tsp, ground)

Cumin (1/4 tsp, ground)

Cardamom (1/4 tsp, ground)

Fresh Rosemary (1 Tbsp)

Fresh Rosemary (12 Sprigs)

Cilantro (1 Bunch)

OTHER

(Check your pantry before shopping as you may already have some of these items)

Extra Virgin Olive Oil (16.5 fl oz)

Honey (2 ½ tsp., optional)

Tomato Raisin Chutney (1 small bottle)

Lemon Juice (3 fl oz)

EQUIPMENT

Chef's knife

Cutting board

Measuring cups and spoons

Mixing bowls

Spatulas

Zester/Small grater

Kitchen Tongs (If using a grill)

2 (18x13-inch) sheet pans

Silicone baking mats or parchment paper

12-inch skillet

8x2-inch baking dish

(if using the oven to broil)

Week 2

Week 2	Breakfast	Lunch	Dinner
Monday	Low-Carb Gluten-Free Pancakes	Hot Spicy Chicken	Sesame-Crusted Tuna with Green Beans
Tuesday	Low-Carb Salmon-Spinach Frittata	Easy Mayo Salmon	Beef Stir Fry
Wednesday	Savory Broccoli Muffins	Zesty Avocado and Lettuce Salad	Herbed Mediterranean Fish Fillet
Thursday	Avocado and Egg Breakfast	Low Carb Chicken Philly Steak	Chicken Tikka with Cauliflower Rice
Friday	Chicken and Vegetable Breakfast Casserole	Beef Burgers	Mushroom Stuffed with Ricotta
Saturday	Pan-Fried Mushrooms, Boiled Eggs, Spinach and Capsicum	Stuffed Zucchini	Chicken Pesto
Sunday	Ground Beef, Eggs and Avocado Breakfast Bowl	Keto Teriyaki Chicken	Slow Cooker Pot Roast with Green Beans

Shopping List

PANTRY

(Check your pantry before shopping as you may already have some of these items)

Black Pepper

Salt

2" Cinnamon Stick (3)

FRESH PRODUCE

Garlic (2 cloves)

Cucumber (12 large)

Tomato (1 large)

Cherry tomatoes (9)

Raspberry (1 cup)

Strawberries (6, hulled and sliced)

Blueberries (1 cup, fresh)

Zucchini (3, medium)

Avocadoes

PROTEIN

Tuna

Ground Beef

Chicken breast

Salmon

Pot Roast

DAIRY

Feta Cheese (3 Tbsp., Low-Fat, Crumbled)

Mozzarella Balls (9 Low-Fat)

Skim Milk (9 Cups)

Greek Yogurt (2 Cups, Plain)

Ricotta cheese (4 oz)

GRAINS, NUTS, SEEDS, AND LEGUMES

(Check your pantry before shopping as you may already have some of these items)

Whole Wheat Bread (10 Slices)

Whole Wheat Couscous (3 Cups, Uncooked)

DRIED/DEHYDRATED FRUITS & VEGETABLES

Raisins and Currants (3/4 Cup)

Dried Apricots (1 ½ Cup)

Sundried Tomatoes (3 tbsp.)

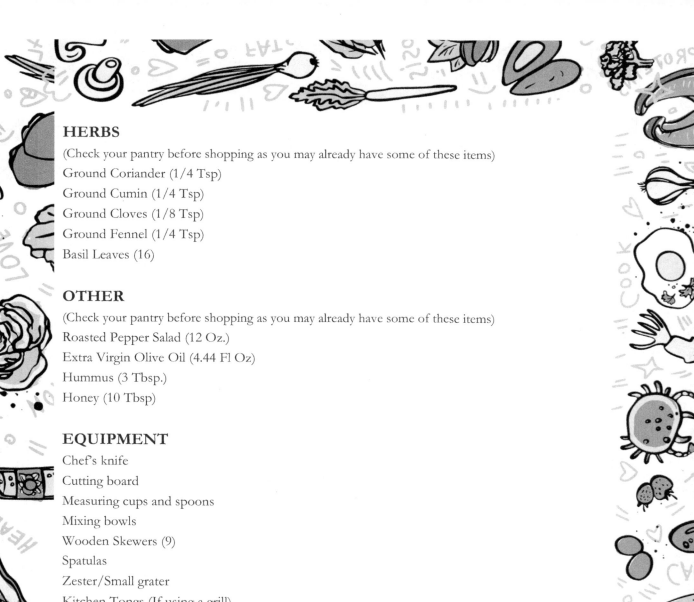

HERBS

(Check your pantry before shopping as you may already have some of these items)

Ground Coriander (1/4 Tsp)

Ground Cumin (1/4 Tsp)

Ground Cloves (1/8 Tsp)

Ground Fennel (1/4 Tsp)

Basil Leaves (16)

OTHER

(Check your pantry before shopping as you may already have some of these items)

Roasted Pepper Salad (12 Oz.)

Extra Virgin Olive Oil (4.44 Fl Oz)

Hummus (3 Tbsp.)

Honey (10 Tbsp)

EQUIPMENT

Chef's knife

Cutting board

Measuring cups and spoons

Mixing bowls

Wooden Skewers (9)

Spatulas

Zester/Small grater

Kitchen Tongs (If using a grill)

2 (18x13-inch) sheet pans

Silicone baking mats or parchment paper

12-inch skillet

8x2-inch baking dish

(if using the oven to broil)

Wood chips

Dutch Oven/Large pot

Wire rack/Oven rack

Vegetable sheer

Week 3

Week 3	Breakfast	Lunch	Dinner
Monday	Low-Carb Gluten-Free Pancakes	Broccoli and Turkey Dish	Salmon and Veggie Parcel
Tuesday	Avocado and Egg Breakfast	Beef Burgers	Garlic Parmesan Chicken Wings
Wednesday	Avocado and Egg Breakfast	Keto Cheese Potato	Bacon and Jalapeno Soup
Thursday	Pan-Fried Mushrooms, Boiled Eggs, Spinach and Capsicum	Easy Bacon Jalapeno Wings	Chicken Pesto
Friday	Egg Salmon Breakfast Bake	Stuffed Zucchini	Herbed Mediterranean Fish Fillet
Saturday	Ground Beef, Eggs and Avocado Breakfast Bowl	Keto Veggie Dish	Beef-Stuffed Mushrooms
Sunday	Savory Broccoli Muffins	Delicious Keto Potato Wedges	Rib Roast

Shopping List

PANTRY

(Check your pantry before shopping as you may already have some of these items)

Stevia Sweetener (2½ Tsp)

Vanilla Extract (1/2 Tsp)

Salt

Pepper

Baking Soda (1/2 Tsp)

Baking Powder (3 Tsp)

Cumin (½ Tbsp.)

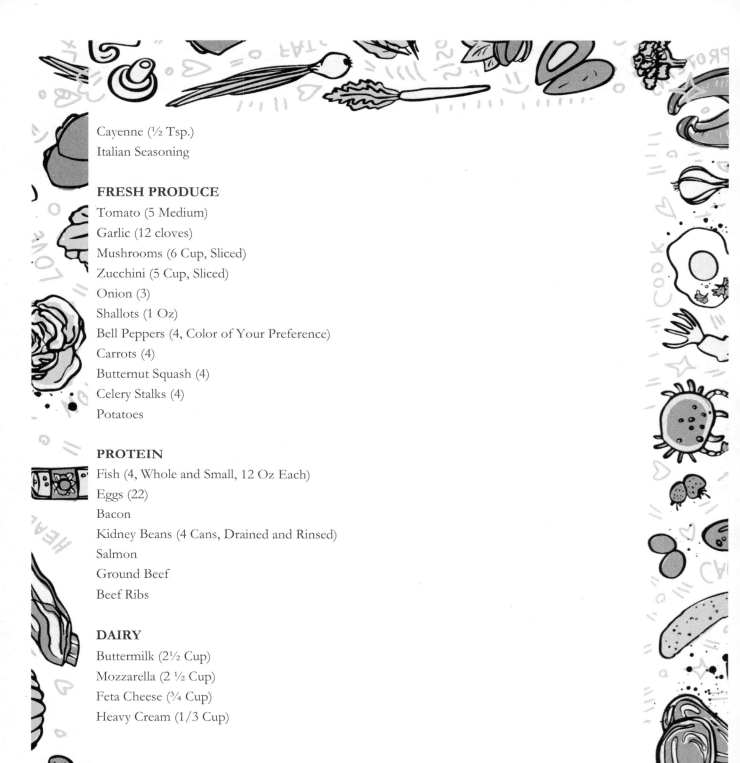

Cayenne (½ Tsp.)

Italian Seasoning

FRESH PRODUCE

Tomato (5 Medium)

Garlic (12 cloves)

Mushrooms (6 Cup, Sliced)

Zucchini (5 Cup, Sliced)

Onion (3)

Shallots (1 Oz)

Bell Peppers (4, Color of Your Preference)

Carrots (4)

Butternut Squash (4)

Celery Stalks (4)

Potatoes

PROTEIN

Fish (4, Whole and Small, 12 Oz Each)

Eggs (22)

Bacon

Kidney Beans (4 Cans, Drained and Rinsed)

Salmon

Ground Beef

Beef Ribs

DAIRY

Buttermilk (2½ Cup)

Mozzarella (2 ½ Cup)

Feta Cheese (¾ Cup)

Heavy Cream (1/3 Cup)

GRAINS, NUTS, SEEDS, AND LEGUMES

(Check your pantry before shopping as you may already have some of these items)

Buckwheat Flour (2 Cups)

Brown Rice (1 ½ Cups, Cooked)

HERBS

(Check your pantry before shopping as you may already have some of these items)

Basil (4¾ Tsp, Dried)

Thyme (1/2 Tsp. Dried)

Coriander (½ Tbsp.)

Parsley (2 Cups, Dried)

Cilantro (1/3 Cup)

Dill (¼ Cup)

Oregano (2 Tsp)

Bay Leaves (7)

OTHER

(Check your pantry before shopping as you may already have some of these items)

Clarified Ghee (2 Tbsp)

Extra Virgin Olive Oil (36¼ Tbsp)

Dry White Wine (3.2 Fl Oz)

Sesame Seeds (1 Tbsp., Toasted)

Tomato Sauce (1 Can)

Tomatoes (2¾ Cups Canned)

Vegetable Broth (7.2 Cups)

EQUIPMENT

Chef's knife

Cutting board

Measuring cups and spoons

Mixing bowls

Wooden Skewers (9)

Spatulas

Zester/Small grater

Kitchen Tongs (If using a grill)

2 (18x13-inch) sheet pans

Silicone baking mats or parchment paper

12-inch skillet

8x2-inch baking dish

(if using the oven to broil)

Week 4

Week 4	Breakfast	Lunch	Dinner
Monday	Pan-Fried Mushrooms, Boiled Eggs, Spinach and Capsicum	Delicious Keto Potato Wedges	Beef Stir Fry
Tuesday	Ground Beef, Eggs and Avocado Breakfast Bowl	Stuffed Zucchini	Crispy Baked Shrimp
Wednesday	Chicken and Vegetable Breakfast Casserole	Keto Cheese Potato	Rib Roast
Thursday	Egg Salmon Breakfast Bake	Easy Bacon Jalapeno Wings	Garlic Salmon
Friday	Savory Broccoli Muffins	Keto Veggie Dish	Grilled Pork with Salsa
Saturday	Avocado and Egg Breakfast	Beef Burgers	Chicken Pesto
Sunday	Low-Carb Gluten-Free Pancakes	Broccoli and Turkey Dish	Garlic Parmesan Chicken Wings

Shopping List

PANTRY

(Check your pantry before shopping as you may already have some of these items)

Sea Salt

Black Pepper

Breadcrumbs (1/4 Cup, Dry)

Paprika (1/2 Tbsp)

FRESH PRODUCE

Banana (2 Small, Peeled)

Strawberries (3 ¼ Cup)

Orange (2)

Roma Tomatoes (5)

Romaine Lettuce (9 Oz)

Arugula (3 Oz)

Bibb Lettuce (2 Oz)

Onion (2 Large, Sliced)

Garlic Clove (2, Minced)

White Mushroom (1 cup)

Baby Spinach (2 Cups)

Eggplant (3 Medium-Sized, Diced)

Zucchini

Potato

Broccoli

Avocado

PROTEIN

Eggs (21)

Chicken breasts (3, boneless and skinless, 5 oz each)

Salmon

Pork

Beef Ribs

Shrimp

DAIRY

Greek Yogurt (1 Cup)

Ricotta Cheese (1 Cup, Fresh)

Feta Cheese (4 Oz, Crumbled)

Mozzarella Cheese (2/3 Cup, Low-Fat and Grated)

Parmesan Cheese (4 Tbsp., Grated)

GRAINS, NUTS, SEEDS, AND LEGUMES

(Check your pantry before shopping as you may already have some of these items)

Flaxseeds (1.5 Tsp)

Sourdough Rye Bread (5 Slice)

Walnut Pieces (1.1 Oz)

Whole Wheat Italian Bread (8 Pieces)

DRIED/DEHYDRATED FRUITS & VEGETABLES

Sundried Tomatoes (2½ Cup, Chopped)

HERBS

(Check your pantry before shopping as you may already have some of these items)

Dried Thyme (1/2 Tbsp)

Dried Basil (4¼ Tbsp)

Cilantro Sprigs (1 Bunch, If Using)

Ground Cumin (½ Tsp)

Ground Coriander (½ Tsp)

OTHER

(Check your pantry before shopping as you may already have some of these items)

Olive Oil (10 Tbsp)

Red Wine Vinaigrette

Fruit Salsa (6 Oz)

EQUIPMENT

Chef's knife

Cutting board

Measuring cups and spoons

Mixing bowls

Wooden Skewers (9)

Spatulas

Zester/Small grater

Kitchen Tongs (If using a grill)

2 (18x13-inch) sheet pans

Silicone baking mats or parchment paper

12-inch skillet

8x2-inch baking dish

(if using the oven to broil)

CHAPTER 13:

KETO BREAKFAST RECIPES

Pan-Fried Mushrooms, Boiled Eggs, Spinach & Capsicum

Preparation Time: 5 minutes

Cooking Time: 10 minutes

Servings: 2

Ingredients

Four large boiled eggs, diced

Two teaspoons extra-virgin olive oil

1/2 cup chopped button mushrooms

1 cup arugula/baby spinach

1/4 cup chopped red onion

1/4 cup chopped green bell pepper

Hot sauce, to serve

Directions

Heat olive oil in a pan set over medium heat; add green bell pepper, onion, and mushrooms and sauté for about 5 minutes or until tender.

Stir in arugula and cook for about 5 minutes or until it wilts; add diced boiled eggs and cook for a few minutes.

Serve right away with hot sauce.

Nutrition

Calories: 201

Total Fat: 14.8g

Carbs: 4.4g

Protein: 13.9g

Ground Beef, Eggs and Avocado Breakfast Bowl

Preparation Time: 10 minutes

Cooking Time: 10 minutes

Servings: 1

Ingredients

Two eggs, lightly beaten

150g ground beef

Eight medium mushrooms, sliced

One red onion, sliced

½ tsp smoked paprika

Salt & pepper

12 pitted black olives, sliced

One small avocado, diced

Directions

Melt coconut oil in a skillet set over medium-high heat; stir in mushrooms, onion, salt, and pepper, and cook for about 3 minutes or until veggies are tender and fragrant.

Stir in smoked paprika and ground beef; cook until beef is no longer pink; transfer to a plate. Add the eggs to the skillet and scramble for a few minutes; add in the beef mixture, olives, and avocado, and cook for about 1 minute. Transfer to a bowl and serve garnished with parsley.

Nutrition

Calories: 559

Total Fat: 47.5g

Carbs: 2.6g

Protein: 30.4g

Low-Carb Gluten-Free Pancakes

Preparation Time: 5 minutes
Cooking Time: 15 minutes
Servings: 3

Ingredients

1/4 cup coconut flour
1 cup blanched almond flour
1/3 cup unsweetened almond milk
Five large eggs
1/4 cup avocado oil
One teaspoon baking powder
1 1/2 teaspoons vanilla extract
1/4 teaspoon sea salt
Three tablespoons stevia
1 cup fresh blueberries for serving

Directions

In a large bowl, whisk together all the ingredients until very smooth.

Heat a pan and then add in oil; drop about three tablespoons of batter into the pan and cook for about 2 minutes. Flip over and cook for 2 minutes more or until lightly browned on both sides. Repeat with the remaining batter.

Serve topped with fresh blueberries.

Nutrition

Calories: 268
Total Fat: 12.4g
Carbs: 6.8g
Protein: 9g

Avocado and Egg Breakfast

Preparation Time: 10 minutes

Cooking Time: 10 minutes

Servings: 1

Ingredients

1/2 avocado, diced

Two hardboiled eggs

Dash of hot sauce

One teaspoon of fresh herbs

Directions

Peel the boiled eggs and rinse with cold water; slice into four pieces each and add to a serving bowl. Add in diced avocado and serve garnished with fresh herbs and drizzled with hot sauce. Enjoy!

Nutrition

Calories: 333

Total Fat: 28.4g

Carbs: 9.8g

Protein: 13.1g

Healthy Lemony Blueberry Pancakes

Preparation Time: 10 minutes

Cooking Time: 10 minutes

Servings: 4

Ingredients

1/3 cup almond flour

Two tablespoons coconut flour

1/4 cup almond milk

1/2 cup blueberries

Two free-range eggs

Three tablespoons lemon juice

1 1/2 teaspoon lemon zest

One tablespoon raw honey

One tablespoon coconut oil

One teaspoon vanilla extract

1/2 teaspoon baking soda

Directions

In a large bowl, whisk together eggs, vanilla, raw honey, and lemon zest until well combined; whisk in coconut flour until well blended. Whisk in almond flour, baking soda, and lemon juice until very smooth.

Heat coconut oil in a skillet set over medium heat; add in two spoonfuls on the batter and spread into a circle. Cook for about 2 minutes per side and then repeat with the remaining ingredients. Divide the fresh blueberries among the pancakes and fold them to make wraps. Serve warm.

Enjoy!

Nutrition

Calories: 134

Total Fat: 8.6g

Carbs: 9.8g

Protein: 4.5g

Cinnamon Berry Shake

Preparation Time: 5 minutes
Cooking Time: 0 minutes
Servings: 4

Ingredients

½ cup blackberries
½ cup blueberries
½ cup raspberries
2 cups of coconut milk
1/4 avocado
One teaspoon cinnamon
One teaspoon liquid stevia
Two tablespoons almond butter

Directions

Blend everything until very smooth. Enjoy!

Nutrition

Calories: 378
Total Fat: 35.8g
Carbs: 5.9g
Protein: 5.3g

Chocolate Coconut & Almond Chia Seed Pudding

Preparation Time: 10 minutes

Cooking Time: 0 minutes

Servings: 4

Ingredients

1 cup of organic coconut cream

1 cup unsweetened almond milk

1/4 liquid stevia

1/4 teaspoon almond extract

1/4 cup chia seeds

Two tablespoons raw cacao powder

A handful of pecans for topping

Directions

In a bowl, whisk together all ingredients, except chia seeds. Refrigerate, covered, for at least 4 hours. Stir in chia seeds and serve topped with raw cacao, raw coconut, and pecans. Enjoy!

Nutrition

Calories: 171

Total Fat: 14.1g

Carbs: 9.7g

Protein: 3.6g

Healthy Keto Coconut Pancakes

Preparation Time: 10 minutes
Cooking Time: 15 minutes
Servings: 3

Ingredients

2 tbsp melted coconut oil

¾ cup coconut milk

½ cup coconut flour

6 eggs

1 tsp baking powder

1 pinch salt

2 tablespoons coconut oil

Directions

Separate the egg whites from yolks, and then, using a hand mixer, whip the egg whites together with salt until stiff peaks form; set aside.

In another bowl, whisk together coconut milk, oil, and yolks until well combined; whisk in baking powder and coconut flour until smooth. Fold egg whites in the batter and let stand for at least 5 minutes.

Melt coconut oil in a nonstick pan and then add batter; spread and cook the pancakes for about 2 minutes per side. Repeat until all the batter is used up.

Serve the pancakes with fresh berries. Enjoy!

Nutrition

Calories: 601

Total Fat: 56.2g

Carbs: 7.3g

Protein: 19.8g

Low-Carb Salmon-Spinach Frittata

Preparation Time: 10 minutes

Cooking Time: 37 minutes

Servings: 4

Ingredients

2 tbsp butter

Eight eggs

1 cup fresh spinach

5 ounces diced smoked salmon

1 cup heavy whipping cream

Salt & pepper

¾ cup shredded cheese

Directions

Preheat your oven to 350 degrees.

Melt butter in a skillet over medium-high heat and then fry salmon for about 7 minutes; stir in spinach until wilted and remove the pan from heat; set aside.

In a small bowl, whisk together cream and eggs until well combined and then pour in a greased baking dish; top with spinach, salmon, and cheese and then bake in the preheated oven for about 30 minutes or until golden brown.

Nutrition

Calories: 559

Total Fat: 47.5g

Carbs: 2.6g

Protein: 30.4g

Sweet Superfood Porridge

Preparation Time: 10 minutes

Cooking Time: 10 minutes

Servings: 4

Ingredients

1½ cups almond milk

Handful chopped almonds or walnuts

Two tablespoon ground flaxseed

Three tablespoon chia seeds

Three tablespoons shredded unsweetened coconut

One teaspoon pure vanilla extract

One scoop protein powder

Toppings

One tablespoon peanut butter

One tablespoon toasted coconut

Directions

In a large bowl, mix all ingredients; refrigerate, covered, overnight. Divide porridge into serving bowls and top with peanut butter and toasted coconut.

Nutrition

Calories: 293

Total Fat: 27.5g

Carbs: 10.7g

Protein: 24.6g

Chicken & Vegetable Breakfast Casserole

Preparation Time: 30 minutes

Cooking Time: 60 minutes

Servings: 6

Ingredients

10 ounce diced chicken, chopped

1 cup diced red onion

1 cup shredded carrots

¾ cup diced bell pepper

2 cups chopped green beans

3 cups spinach

1 cup of water

12 free-range eggs, beaten

One teaspoon sea salt

½ teaspoon pepper

Directions

Preheat oven to 350°F.

Coat a 9x13-inch casserole dish with olive oil cooking spray and set aside.

Cook chicken in a skillet over medium heat for about 10 minutes or until crispy; stir in red onions, carrots, bell pepper, and green beans and continue cooking for about 5 minutes or until veggies are tender. Stir in spinach and cook for 2 minutes or until wilted; remove from heat.

In a blender, blend with water, eggs, and salt and well combined.

Transfer the vegetable mixture to the casserole and cover with egg mixture; stir well and bake for about 60 minutes or until eggs are set.

Nutrition

Calories: 417

Total Fat: 28.5g

Carbs: 9.4g

Protein: 30.2g

Low Carb Key Lime Cashew & Spinach Smoothie

Preparation Time: 5 minutes
Cooking Time: 0 minutes
Servings: 2

Ingredients
1/4 cup cashews, soaked
2 cups coconut milk
4 tablespoons lime juice
2 tablespoons chia seeds
2 tablespoons coconut butter
2 handfuls spinach
1/2 avocado
1 tablespoon lime zest
20 drops liquid stevia
½ teaspoon vanilla extract
2 tablespoons collagen

Directions
Combine all ingredients in a blender and blend until very smooth. Enjoy!

Nutrition
Calories: 340
Total Fat: 21g
Carbs: 17g
Protein: 12g

Tasty Breakfast Wrap

Preparation Time: 10 minutes
Cooking Time: 40 minutes
Servings: 1

Ingredients

Two multi-grain flax wraps
Three egg whites
1 ½ tbsp. extra virgin olive oil
¼ cup sun-dried tomatoes
¼ cup fresh spinach, chopped
¼ cup crumbled feta cheese
Sea salt and freshly ground pepper to taste

Directions

Heat the oil in a nonstick pan and sauté the tomatoes, spinach, and egg whites until almost done, then flip and cook the other side.

Add the crumbled feta to warm it up. Sprinkle with salt and pepper, then remove from heat.

Heat the wraps on a dry pan, then serve the egg mixture into the wraps and roll them up.

Enjoy!

Nutrition

Calories: 391
Total Fat: 33.1g
Carbs: 17.4g
Protein: 17.7g

Egg Salmon Breakfast Bake

Preparation Time: 10 minutes

Cooking Time: 47 minutes

Servings: 6

Ingredients

6 ounces smoked wild-caught salmon, skinless, sliced into 1/2-inch pieces

Two tablespoons extra virgin olive oil

One red onion sliced crosswise

1 cup red peppers, chopped

1 cup mushrooms

Eight large eggs

1 cup kefir

One teaspoon nutmeg

One tablespoon chopped fresh dill

¼ teaspoon sea salt

¼ teaspoon black pepper

¾ cup goat cheese, crumbled

Directions

Preheat oven to 350°F.

Heat extra virgin olive oil in a sauté pan set over medium-high heat; stir in peppers and red onion. Sauté, stirring, for about 3 minutes or until onion is tender and fragrant. Stir in mushrooms and cook for about 4 minutes or until lightly browned and tender. Remove the pan from heat.

Spread the mushroom mixture into a greased baking dish and top with salmon.

In a bowl, beat together eggs, kefir, nutmeg, dill, salt, and pepper; pour over the salmon mixture and bake for about 40 minutes. Remove from oven and top with goat cheese to serve.

Nutrition

Calories: 320 Total Fat: 22.9g

Carbs: 5.9g Dietary Fiber: 1.1g

Sugars: 3.5g Protein: 23.4g Cholesterol: 284mg

Sodium: 841mg

Savory Broccoli Muffins

Preparation Time: 15 minutes
Cooking Time: 20 minutes
Servings: 2

Ingredients

Two tablespoons unsalted butter
Six large organic eggs
½ cup heavy whipping cream
½ cup Parmesan cheese, grated
Salt and ground black pepper, as required
1¼ cups broccoli, chopped
Two tablespoons fresh parsley, chopped
½ cup Swiss cheese, grated

Directions

Preheat your oven to 350 F (180 C). Grease 12 cups of a muffin tin.

In a bowl, add the eggs, cream, Parmesan cheese, salt, and black pepper and beat until well combined.

Divide the broccoli and parsley in the bottom of each prepared muffin cup evenly.

Top with the egg mixture, followed by the Swiss cheese.

Bake for about 20 minutes, rotating the pan once halfway through.

Remove from the oven and place onto a wire rack for about 5 minutes before serving.

Carefully invert the muffins onto a serving platter and serve warm.

Nutrition

Calories: 103
Fat: 8.3g
Sat Fat: 4.4g
Cholesterol: 112mg
Sodium: 103mg
Protein: 6.1g
Carbs: 10g

CHAPTER 14:

LUNCH RECIPES

Beef Burgers

Preparation Time: 15 minutes
Cooking Time: 6 minutes
Servings: 4

Ingredients

8 ounces grass-fed ground beef
Salt and ground black pepper, as required
1-ounce mozzarella cheese, cubed
One tablespoon unsalted butter

Yogurt Sauce

1/3 cup plain Greek yogurt
One teaspoon fresh lemon juice
¼ teaspoon garlic, minced
Salt, as required
½ teaspoon granulated erythritol

Directions

In a bowl, add the beef, salt, and black pepper, and mix until well combined.
Make two equal-sized patties from the mixture.
Place mozzarella cube inside of each patty and cover with the beef.
In a frying pan, melt butter over medium heat and cook the patties for about 2–3 minutes per side.
Divide the greens onto serving plates and top each with one patty.
Serve immediately.
Meanwhile, for the yogurt sauce: place all the ingredients in a serving bowl and mix until well.
Divide patties onto each serving plate and serve alongside the yogurt sauce.

Nutrition

Calories 322 Carbs 3.5g
Fat 19.8g Protein 29.5g

Keto Cheese Potato

Preparation Time: 5 minutes
Cooking Time: 15 minutes
Servings: 2

Ingredients

One large turnip, peeled, diced
Two slices of bacon, chopped
One tablespoon olive oil
One tablespoon softened cream cheese
1/4 of spring onion, diced, and more for garnishing

Directions

Bring out a skillet pan, place it over medium-high heat, add oil and when hot, add diced turnip, season with salt, black pepper, and paprika, sprinkle with garlic, stir well and cook for 5 minutes.

Then add onion, stir and continue cooking for 3 minutes until onions start to soften.

Add chopped bacon, continue cooking for 5 to 7 minutes, or until bacon is crispy and remove the pan from heat.

Top with green onions and cream cheese, and then serve.

Nutrition

Calories: 88
Fat: 9g
Protein: 3g
Carbs: 3.5g
Fiber: 1g

Keto Veggie Dish

Preparation Time: 5 minutes
Cooking Time: 5 minutes
Servings: 2

Ingredients

¼ teaspoon salt

1 ½ teaspoon minced garlic

1 tablespoon coconut oil

8 ounces spinach leaves

Directions

Bring out a frying pan, place it over medium heat, add oil and when hot, add spinach and cook for 5 minutes until its leaves wilts.

Then add garlic and salt, stir well and continue cooking for 2 minutes.

Nutrition

Calories: 155

Fat: 14g

Protein: 4g

Carbs: 2g

Fiber: 6g

Delicious Keto Potato Wedges

Preparation Time: 5 minutes
Cooking Time: 20 minutes
Servings: 2

Ingredients

½ teaspoon garlic powder
¾ teaspoon onion powder
1 ½ tablespoon melted coconut oil
1 tablespoon cream cheese
2 large turnips

Directions

Turn on the oven, then set it to 350°F, and let it preheat.

Prepare taco seasoning, and for this, stir together salt, onion powder, garlic powder, red chili powder, cumin, and oregano and set aside until required.

Peel the turnips, cut into wedges, place them in a plastic bag, add prepared taco seasoning, add oil, seal the bag, and turn it upside down until well-coated.

Transfer the mixture onto a baking sheet, spread the wedges evenly, and bake for 20 minutes until golden brown and cooked.

Nutrition

Calories: 129
Fat: 12.6g
Protein: 1.7g
Carbs: 4.3g
Fiber: 2.2g

Easy Bacon Jalapeno Rings

Preparation Time: 5 minutes

Cooking Time: 10 minutes

Servings: 2

Ingredients

¼ teaspoon salt

1/8 teaspoon ground black pepper

Four jalapeno peppers

4 ounces cream cheese

Eight strips of bacon

Directions

Turn on the oven, then set it to 400°F and let it preheat.

In the meantime, cut each pepper in half lengthwise, remove and discard the seeds and then fill the peppers with cream cheese.

Wrap each pepper with bacon and cook for 10 minutes until peppers are tender and bacon is nicely golden brown.

Nutrition

Calories: 78.5

Fat: 4g

Protein: 1.5g

Carbs: 1.3g

Fiber: 0.2g

Hot Spicy Chicken

Preparation Time: 5 minutes
Cooking Time: 25 minutes
Servings: 2

Ingredients

¼ tablespoon fennel seeds, ground
¼ teaspoon smoked paprika
½ teaspoon hot paprika
½ teaspoon minced garlic
2 chicken thighs, boneless

Directions

Turn on the oven, then set it to 325°F and let it preheat.

Prepare the spice mix and for this, bring out a small bowl, add all the ingredients in it, except for chicken, and stir until well mixed.

Brush the mixture on all sides of the chicken, rub it well into the meat, then place chicken onto a baking sheet and roast for 15 to 25 minutes until thoroughly cooked, basting every 10 minutes with the drippings.

Nutrition

Calories: 102.3
Fat: 8g
Protein: 7.2g
Carbs: 0.3g
Fiber: 0.3g

Broccoli and Turkey Dish

Preparation Time: 5 minutes

Cooking Time: 15 minutes

Servings: 2

Ingredients

¼ teaspoon red pepper flakes

One tablespoon olive oil

One teaspoon soy sauce

4 ounces broccoli florets

4 ounces cauliflower florets, riced

4 ounces ground turkey

Directions

Bring out a skillet pan, place it over medium heat, add olive oil, and when hot, add beef, crumble it and cook for 8 minutes until no longer pink.

Then add broccoli florets and riced cauliflower, stir well, drizzle with soy sauce and sesame oil, season with salt, black pepper, and red pepper flakes and continue cooking 5 minutes until vegetables have thoroughly cooked.

Nutrition

Calories: 120.3

Fat: 8.3g

Protein: 8.4g

Carbs: 2g

Fiber: 1g

Easy Mayo Salmon

Preparation Time: 5 minutes

Cooking Time: 10 minutes

Servings: 2

Ingredients

2 salmon fillets

4 tablespoons mayonnaise

Directions

Turn on the panini press, spray it with oil and let it preheat.

Then spread one tablespoon of mayonnaise on each side of the salmon, place them on panini press pan, shut with lid, and cook for 7 to 10 minutes until salmon has cooked to the desired level.

Nutrition

Calories: 132.7

Fat: 11.1g

Protein: 8g

Carbs: 0.3g

Zesty Avocado and Lettuce Salad

Preparation Time: 5 minutes

Cooking Time: 0 minutes

Servings: 2

Ingredients

½ of a lime, juiced

One avocado, pitted, sliced

Two tablespoons olive oil

4 ounces chopped lettuce

Four tablespoons chopped chives

Directions

Prepare the dressing and for this, bring out a small bowl, add oil, lime juice, salt, and black pepper, stir until mixed, and then slowly mix oil until combined.

Bring out a large bowl, add avocado, lettuce, and chives, and then toss gently.

Drizzle with dressing, toss until well coated, and then serve.

Nutrition

Calories: 125.7

Fat: 11g

Protein: 1.3g

Carbs: 1.7g

Fiber: 3.7g

Veggie, Bacon, and Egg Dish

Preparation Time: 5 minutes
Cooking Time: 5 minutes
Servings: 2

Ingredients

¼ cup mayonnaise
Two eggs, boiled, sliced
4 ounces spinach
Four slices of bacon, chopped

Directions

Bring out a skillet pan, place it over medium heat, add bacon, and cook for 5 minutes until browned.

In the meantime, bring out a salad bowl, add spinach to it, top with bacon and eggs and drizzle with mayonnaise.

Toss until well mixed and then serve.

Nutrition

Calories: 181.5
Fat: 16.7g
Protein: 7.3g
Carbs: 1.2g
Fiber: 0.3g

Keto Teriyaki Chicken

Preparation Time: 5 minutes

Cooking Time: 18 minutes

Servings: 2

Ingredients

1 tablespoon olive oil

1 tablespoon swerve sweetener

2 chicken thighs, boneless

2 tablespoons soy sauce

Directions

Bring out a skillet pan, place it over medium heat, add oil and when hot, add chicken thighs and cook for 5 minutes per side until seared.

Drizzle the chicken thighs with soy sauce and bring the sauce to boil.

Switch heat to medium-low level, continue cooking for 3 minutes until chicken is evenly glazed, and then transfer to a plate.

Serve chicken with cauliflower rice.

Nutrition

Calories: 150

Fat: 9g

Protein: 17.3g

Carbs: 1g

Lime Chicken with Coleslaw

Preparation Time: 35 minutes
Cooking Time: 8 minutes
Servings: 2

Ingredients

¼ teaspoon minced garlic
½ of a lime, juiced, zested
¾ tablespoon apple cider vinegar
One chicken thigh, boneless
2 ounces coleslaw

Directions

Prepare the marinade and for this, bring out a medium bowl, add vinegar, oil, garlic, paprika, salt, lime juice, and zest and stir until well mixed.

Cut chicken thighs into bite-size pieces, toss until well mixed, and marinate it in the refrigerator for 30 minutes.

Then Bring out a skillet pan, place it over medium-high heat, add butter and marinated chicken pieces and cook for 8 minutes until golden brown and thoroughly cooked.

Serve chicken with coleslaw.

Nutrition

Calories: 157.3
Fat: 12.8g
Protein: 9g
Carbs: 1g

Low Carb Chicken Philly Cheesesteak

Preparation Time: 10 minutes

Cooking Time: 15 minutes

Servings: 3

Ingredients

3 slices provolone cheese

½ teaspoon minced garlic

½ cup bell pepper, diced, fresh or frouncesen

½ cup diced onion, fresh or frouncesen

Two teaspoons olive oil, divided

One dash ground pepper

½ teaspoon garlic powder

½ teaspoon onion powder

Two tablespoons Worcestershire sauce

10 ounces about two boneless chicken breasts

Directions

Cut the chicken into thin cuts, then place in a freezer for a few minutes to make it easier to make this recipe. Put the chicken in a bowl and add in Worcestershire sauce, onion powder, garlic powder, and pepper; toss to coat well with the chicken. In an ovenproof pan, put one teaspoon of olive oil, add in the chicken, and cook for around 5 minutes or turn brown. Turn the chicken pieces to the other side and cook for another 2-3 minutes, until brown.

Remove from the pan.

Put the left olive oil in the same pan, then add garlic, pepper, and onions.

Cook while constantly stirring for about 2-3 minutes until they are hot and soft.

Reduce the heat and put the chicken pieces back into the pan; stir to combine everything.

Put the cheese on top and cover with a lid for another 2-3 minutes until the cheese melts. Serve in bowls and enjoy.

Nutrition

Calories: 263 Fat: 13g Carbs: 5g Protein: 27g Fiber: 0.3g

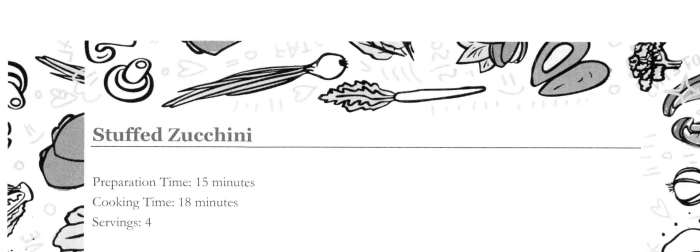

Stuffed Zucchini

Preparation Time: 15 minutes
Cooking Time: 18 minutes
Servings: 4

Ingredients

Four medium zucchinis halved lengthwise
1 cup red bell pepper, seeded and minced
½ cup Kalamata olives, pitted and minced
½ cup fresh tomatoes, minced
One teaspoon garlic, minced
One tablespoon dried oregano, crushed
Salt, and ground black pepper, as required
½ cup feta cheese, crumbled

Directions

Preheat your oven to 350°F.

Grease a large baking sheet.

With a melon baller, scoop out the flesh of each zucchini half. Discard the flesh.

In a bowl, mix the bell pepper, olives, tomatoes, garlic, oregano, salt, and black pepper.

Stuff each zucchini half with the veggie mixture evenly.

Arrange zucchini halves onto the prepared baking sheet and bake for about 15 minutes.

Now, set the oven to broiler on high.

Top each zucchini half with feta cheese and broil for about 3 minutes.

Serve hot.

Nutrition

Calories: 59
Carbs: 4.3g
Total Fat: 3.2g
Protein: 2.9g

Taco Meat

Preparation Time: 5 minutes
Cooking Time: 8 minutes
Servings: 8

Ingredients

Ground turkey – 2-pound
Diced white onion – 1/2 cup
Diced red bell pepper – 1/2 cup
Tomato sauce, unsalted – 1 cup
Taco seasoning – 1 1 /2 tablespoon
Fajita seasoning – 1 ½ tablespoon
Avocado oil – 1 teaspoon

Directions

Switch on the instant pot, grease pot with oil, press the 'sauté/simmer' button, wait until the oil is hot, add the ground turkey and cook for 7 to 10 minutes or until nicely browned.

Then add remaining ingredients, stir until mixed and press the 'keep warm' button.

Shut the instant pot with its lid in the sealed position, then press the 'manual' button, press '+/-' to set the cooking time to 8 minutes and cook at a high-pressure setting; when the pressure builds in the pot, the cooking timer will start.

When the instant pot buzzes, press the 'keep warm' button, do a quick pressure release and open the lid.

Transfer taco meat to a bowl, top with avocado slices, garnish with cilantro, and serve.

Nutrition

Calories: 231
Fat: 14g
Protein: 21g
Carbs: 2.5g
Fiber: 1.5g

CHAPTER 15:

DINNER RECIPES

Sesame-Crusted Tuna with Green Beans

Preparation Time: 15 minutes

Cooking Time: 5 minutes

Servings: 4

Ingredients

¼ cup white sesame seeds

¼ cup black sesame seeds

4 (6-ounce) ahi tuna steaks

Salt and pepper

One tablespoon olive oil

One tablespoon coconut oil

2 cups green beans

Directions

Combine the two types of sesame seeds in a shallow dish.

Season the tuna with salt and pepper.

Dredge the tuna in the sesame seed mixture.

Heat the olive oil in a skillet to high heat, then add the tuna.

Cook for 1 to 2 minutes until seared, then turn and sear on the other side.

Remove the tuna from the skillet and let the tuna rest while reheating the coconut oil skillet.

Fry the green beans in the oil for 5 minutes, then serve with sliced tuna.

Nutrition

Calories: 380

Fat: 19g

Protein: 44.5g

Carbs: 8g

Fiber: 8g

Chicken Tikka with Cauliflower Rice

Preparation Time: 10 minutes

Cooking Time: 6n hours

Servings: 4

Ingredients

2 pounds boneless chicken thighs, chopped

1 cup of canned coconut milk

1 cup heavy cream

Three tablespoons tomato paste

Two tablespoons garam masala

One tablespoon fresh grated ginger

One tablespoon minced garlic

One tablespoon smoked paprika

Two teaspoons onion powder

One teaspoon guar gum

One tablespoon butter

1 ½ cup riced cauliflower

Directions

Spread the chicken in a slow cooker, then stir in the remaining ingredients except for the cauliflower and butter.

Cover and cook on low heat for 6 hours until the chicken is done and the sauce thickened.

Melt the butter in a saucepan over medium-high heat.

Add the riced cauliflower and cook for 6 to 8 minutes until tender.

Serve the chicken tikka with the cauliflower rice.

Nutrition

Calories: 485 Fat: 32g

Protein: 43g Carbs: 6.5g Fiber: 1g

Grilled Salmon and Zucchini

Preparation Time: 5 minutes
Cooking Time: 10 minutes
Servings: 4

Ingredients

4 (6-ounces) boneless salmon fillets
One tablespoon olive oil
Salt and pepper
One large zucchini, sliced into coins
Two tablespoons fresh lemon juice
¼ cup fresh chopped cilantro
One teaspoon lemon zest
½ cup of canned coconut milk

Directions

Preheat a grill pan to high heat and spray liberally with cooking spray.
Brush the salmon with olive oil and season with salt and pepper.
Toss the zucchini with lemon juice and season with salt and pepper.
Place the salmon fillets and zucchini on the grill pan.
Cook for 5 minutes, then turn everything and cook 5 minutes more.
Combine the remaining ingredients in a blender and blend into a sauce.
Serve the salmon fillets drizzled with the zucchini on the side.

Nutrition

Calories: 350
Fat: 21.5g
Protein: 35g
Carbs: 8g
Fiber: 2g

Slow-Cooker Pot Roast with Green Beans

Preparation Time: 10 minutes
Cooking Time: 8 hours
Servings: 8

Ingredients

Two medium stalks celery, sliced
One medium yellow onion, chopped
1 (3-pound) boneless beef chuck roast
Salt and pepper
¼ cup beef broth
Two tablespoons Worcestershire sauce
4 cups green beans, trimmed
Two tablespoons cold butter, chopped

Directions

Combine the celery and onion in a slow cooker.
Place the roast on top and season liberally with salt and pepper.
Whisk together the beef broth and Worcestershire sauce, then pour it in.
Cover and cook on low heat for 8 hours until the beef is very tender.
Remove the beef to a cutting board and cut it into chunks.
Return the beef to the slow cooker and add the beans and chopped butter.
Cover and cook on high for 20 to 30 minutes until the beans are tender.

Nutrition

Calories: 375
Fat: 13.5g
Protein: 53g
Carbs: 6g
Fiber: 2g

Salmon & Veggie Parcel

Preparation Time: 15 minutes

Cooking Time: 20 minutes

Servings: 2

Ingredients

6 (3-ounce) salmon fillets

Salt and ground black pepper, as required

One yellow bell pepper, seeded and cubed

One red bell pepper, seeded and cubed

Four plum tomatoes, cubed

One small yellow onion, sliced thinly

½ cup fresh parsley, chopped

¼ cup olive oil

Two tablespoons fresh lemon juice

Directions

Preheat your oven to 400 F (200 C).

Arrange six pieces of foil onto a smooth surface.

Place one salmon fillet onto each foil paper and sprinkle with salt and black pepper.

In a bowl, add the bell peppers, tomato, and onion, and mix.

Place veggie mixture over each fillet evenly and top with parsley and capers.

Drizzle with oil and lemon juice.

Fold the foil around the salmon mixture to seal it.

Arrange the foil packets onto a large baking sheet in a single layer.

Bake for about 20 minutes.

Serve hot.

Nutrition

Calories: 224 Fat: 14g Saturated fat: 2g

Cholesterol: 38mg Sodium: 811mg Carbs: 8.7g Fiber: 1.9g Sugar: 5.9g Protein: 18.2g

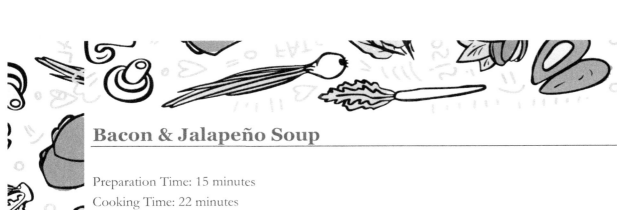

Bacon & Jalapeño Soup

Preparation Time: 15 minutes

Cooking Time: 22 minutes

Servings: 1

Ingredients

¼ cup unsalted butter

Four medium jalapeño peppers, seeded and chopped

One small yellow onion, chopped

One teaspoon dried thyme, crushed

½ teaspoon ground cumin

3 cups homemade chicken broth

8 ounces cheddar cheese, shredded

¾ cup heavy cream

Salt and ground black pepper, as required

Six cooked bacon slices, chopped

Directions

In a large pan, melt one tablespoon of the butter over medium heat and sauté the jalapeño peppers for about 1-2 minutes.

With a slotted spoon, transfer the jalapeño peppers onto a plate.

In the same pan, melt the remaining butter over medium heat and sauté the onion for about 3-4 minutes. Add the spices and sauté for about 1 minute.

Add the broth and bring to a boil. Reduce the heat to low and cook for about 10 minutes.

Remove from the heat, and with an immersion blender, blend until smooth.

Return the pan over medium-low heat.

Stir in ¾ of the cooked bacon, cooked jalapeño, cheese, cream, and black pepper, and cook for about 5 minutes. Serve hot with the topping of the remaining bacon.

Nutrition

Calories: 549 Fat: 46.5g Saturated fat: 24.6g Cholesterol: 135mg

Sodium: 1900mg Carbs: 4.5g Fiber: 0.9g Sugar: 1.7g Protein: 27.9g

Beef-Stuffed Mushrooms

Preparation Time: 20 minutes
Cooking Time: 25 minutes
Servings: 4

Ingredients

Four mushrooms stemmed
Three tablespoons olive oil, divided
One yellow onion, sliced thinly
One red bell pepper, sliced into strips
One green bell pepper, sliced into strips
Salt and pepper to taste
8 ounces. beef, sliced thinly
3 ounces. provolone cheese, sliced
Chopped parsley

Directions

Preheat your oven to 350°F.
Arrange the mushrooms on a baking pan.
Brush with oil. Add the remaining oil to a pan over medium heat.
Cook the onion and bell peppers for 5 minutes.
Season with salt and pepper. Place onion mixture on a plate.
Cook the beef in the pan for 5 minutes.
Sprinkle with salt and pepper.
Add the onion mixture back to the pan.
Mix well. Fill the mushrooms with the beef mixture and cheese.
Bake in the oven for 15 minutes.

Nutrition

Calories: 333 Fat: 20.3g
Carbs: 8.2g Fiber: 3.7g Protein: 25.2g

Rib Roast

Preparation Time: 10 minutes
Cooking Time 3 hours
Servings: 8

Ingredients

1 rib roast
Salt to taste
12 cloves garlic, chopped
2 teaspoons lemon zest
6 tablespoons fresh rosemary, chopped
5 sprigs thyme

Directions

Preheat your oven to 325°F.
Season all sides of the rib roast with salt.
Place the rib roast in a baking pan.
Sprinkle with garlic, lemon zest, and rosemary.
Add herb sprigs on top.
Roast for 3 hours.
Let rest for a few minutes, and then slice and serve.

Nutrition

Calories: 329
Fat: 27g
Carbs: 5.3g
Fiber: 1.8g
Protein: 18g

Beef Stir Fry

Preparation Time:
Cooking Time:
Servings:

Ingredients

One tablespoon soy sauce

One tablespoon ginger, minced

One teaspoon glucomannan powder

One teaspoon dry sherry

12 ounces. beef, sliced into strips

One teaspoon toasted sesame oil

Two tablespoons oyster sauce

1 lb. baby bok choy, sliced

Three tablespoons chicken broth

Directions

Mix soy sauce, ginger, glucomannan powder, and dry sherry in a bowl.

Toss the beef in the mixture.

Pour oil into a pan over medium heat.

Cook the beef for 5 minutes, stirring.

Add oyster sauce, bok choy, and chicken broth to the pan.

Cook for 1 minute.

Nutrition

Calories: 247

Fat: 15.8g

Carbs: 6.3g

Fiber: 1.1g

Protein: 25g

Grilled Pork with Salsa

Preparation Time: 30 minutes
Cooking Time: 15 minutes
Servings: 4

Ingredients

One onion, chopped
One tomato, chopped
One tablespoon olive oil
One tablespoon lime juice
Two tablespoons fresh cilantro, chopped
Salt and pepper to taste
Pork
1 lb. pork tenderloin, sliced
One tablespoon olive oil
Salt and pepper to taste
½ teaspoon ground cumin
¾ teaspoon chili powder

Directions

Combine salsa ingredients in a bowl.
Cover and refrigerate.
Brush pork tenderloin with oil.
Season with salt, pepper, cumin, and chili powder.
Grill pork for 5 to 7 minutes per side.
Slice pork and serve with salsa.

Nutrition

Calories: 219 Fat: 9.5g
Carbs: 8.3g Fiber: 1.5g
Protein: 24g

Chicken Pesto

Preparation Time: 15 minutes
Cooking Time: 25 minutes
Servings: 4

Ingredients

1 lb. chicken cutlet
Salt and pepper to taste
One tablespoon olive oil
½ cup onion, chopped
½ cup heavy cream
½ cup dry white wine
One tomato, chopped
¼ cup pesto
Two tablespoons basil, chopped

Directions

Season chicken with salt and pepper.
Pour oil into a pan over medium heat.
Cook chicken for 3 to 4 minutes per side.
Place the chicken on a plate.
Add the onion to the pan.
Cook for 1 minute.
Stir in the rest of the ingredients.
Bring to a boil.
Simmer for 15 minutes.
Put the chicken back in the pan.
Cook for two more minutes and then serve.

Nutrition

Calories: 371 Fat: 23.7g
Carbs: 5.7g Fiber: 1g Protein: 27.7g

Garlic Parmesan Chicken Wings

Preparation Time: 20 minutes
Cooking Time: 20 minutes
Servings: 8

Ingredients

Cooking spray
½ cup all-purpose flour
Pepper to taste
Two tablespoons garlic powder
Three eggs, beaten
One ¼ cups Parmesan cheese, grated
2 cups breadcrumbs
2 lb. chicken wings

Directions

Preheat your oven to 450°F.
Spray baking pan with oil.
In a bowl, mix the flour, pepper, and garlic powder.
Add eggs to another bowl.
Mix the Parmesan cheese and breadcrumbs in another bowl.
Dip the chicken wings in the first, second, and third bowls.
Spray chicken wings with oil.
Bake in the oven for 20 minutes.

Nutrition

Calories: 221
Fat: 11.6g
Carbs: 8g
Fiber: 0.4g
Protein: 16g

Crispy Baked Shrimp

Preparation Time: 15 minutes

Cooking Time: 10 minutes

Servings: 4

Ingredients

¼ cup panko breadcrumbs

Three tablespoons olive oil, divided

1 ½ lb. jumbo shrimp, peeled and deveined

Salt and pepper to taste

Two tablespoons lemon juice

One tablespoon garlic, chopped

Two tablespoons butter

¼ cup Parmesan cheese, grated

Two tablespoons chives, chopped

Directions

Preheat your oven to 425°F.

Add panko breadcrumbs to a pan over medium heat.

Cook until toasted.

Transfer to a plate.

Coat baking pan with one tablespoon oil.

Arrange shrimp in a single layer in a baking pan.

Season with salt and pepper.

Mix the lemon juice, garlic, and butter in a bowl.

Pour mixture on top of the shrimp.

Add Parmesan cheese and chives to the breadcrumbs.

Sprinkle breadcrumbs on top of the shrimp.

Bake for 10 minutes.

Nutrition

Calories: 340 Fat: 18.7g Carbs: 6g Fiber: 0.8g Protein: 36.9g

Herbed Mediterranean Fish Fillet

Preparation Time: 20 minutes
Cooking Time   1 hour
Servings: 6

Ingredients

3 lb. sea bass fillet
Salt to taste
Two tablespoons tarragon, chopped
¼ cup dry white wine
Three tablespoons olive oil, divided
One tablespoon butter
Two cloves garlic, minced
Two cups whole-wheat breadcrumbs
Three tablespoons parsley, chopped
Three tablespoons oregano, chopped
Three tablespoons fresh basil, chopped

Directions

Preheat your oven to 350°F.
Season fish with salt and tarragon.
Pour half of the oil into a roasting pan.
Stir in wine.
Add the fish to the roasting pan.
Bake in the oven for 50 minutes.
Add remaining oil to a pan over medium heat.
Cook the herbs, breadcrumbs, and salt.
Spread breadcrumb mixture on top of fish and bake for 5 minutes.

Nutrition

Calories: 288 Fat: 12.7g Carbs: 10.4g Fiber: 1.8g Protein: 29.5g

Mushroom Stuffed with Ricotta

Preparation Time: 10 minutes

Cooking Time: 10 minutes

Servings: 4

Ingredients

Four large mushrooms stemmed

One tablespoon olive oil

Salt and pepper to taste

¼ cup basil, chopped

1 cup ricotta cheese

¼ cup Parmesan cheese, grated

Directions

Preheat your grill.

Coat the mushrooms with oil.

Season with salt and pepper.

Grill for 5 minutes.

Stuff each mushroom with a mixture of basil, ricotta cheese, and Parmesan cheese.

Grill for another 5 minutes.

Nutrition

Calories: 259

Fat: 17.3g

Carbs: 14.9g

Fiber: 2.6g

Protein: 12.2g

CHAPTER 16:

SEAFOOD & FISH RECIPES

Flavors Cioppino

Preparation Time: 10 minutes

Cooking Time: 5 minutes

Servings: 6

Ingredients

1 lb codfish, cut into chunks

1 1/2 lbs shrimp

28 oz can of tomatoes, diced

1 cup dry white wine

One bay leaf

1 tsp cayenne

1 tsp oregano

One shallot, chopped

1 tsp garlic, minced

1 tbsp olive oil

1/2 tsp salt

Directions

Add oil into the inner pot of the instant pot and set the pot on sauté mode.

Add shallot and garlic and sauté for 2 minutes.

Add wine, bay leaf, cayenne, oregano, and salt and cook for 3 minutes.

Add remaining ingredients and stir well.

Seal the pot with a lid, select manual, and cook on low for 0 minutes.

Once done, release pressure using quick release. Remove lid.

Serve and enjoy.

Nutrition

Calories: 281 Fat: 5g

Carbs: 10.5g Sugar: 4.9g

Protein: 40.7g Cholesterol: 266mg

Garlicky Parmesan Salmon with Asparagus

Preparation Time: 10 minutes

Cooking Time: 15 minutes

Servings: 2

Ingredients

2 (6-ounce / 170-g) salmon fillets, skin on and patted dry

Pink Himalayan salt, to taste

Freshly ground black pepper, to taste

1 pound (454 g) fresh asparagus, ends snapped off

Three tablespoons butter

Two minced garlic cloves

¼ cup Parmesan cheese, shredded

Directions

Preheat the oven to 400°F (205°C). Line a baking pan with aluminum foil and set it aside.

In a bowl, rub the salmon fillets with salt and pepper.

Arrange the seasoned salmon fillets in the baking pan's center and spread the asparagus around the fillets. Set aside.

Melt the butter in a skillet over medium heat. Toss in the garlic cloves and cook for about 3 minutes until fragrant, stirring constantly.

Pour the butter mixture over the salmon fillets and asparagus. Scatter the Parmesan cheese on top.

Bake in the preheated oven for 12 minutes, or until the fish flakes easily with a fork and the asparagus is fork tender.

Remove from the oven and serve hot.

Nutrition

Calories: 430

Fat: 26.3g

Protein: 42.2g

Carbs: 6.2g

Fiber: 5.1g

Fried Pork Rind Crusted Salmon Cake

Preparation Time: 10 minutes

Cooking Time: 12 minutes

Servings: 4

Ingredients

6 ounces (170 g) canned Alaska wild salmon, drained

One egg, lightly beaten

Two tablespoons pork rinds, crushed

Three tablespoons mayonnaise, divided

Pink Himalayan salt, to taste

Freshly ground black pepper, to taste

Mayo Sauce

One tablespoon ghee

½ tablespoon Dijon mustard

Directions

Mix the salmon, beaten egg, pork rinds, 1½ tablespoons mayo, salt, and pepper in a large bowl until well combined.

Make the salmon cakes: On a lightly floured surface, scoop out two tablespoons of the salmon mixture and shape into a patty with your palm, about ½ inch thick. Repeat with the remaining salmon mixture.

Melt the ghee in a large skillet over medium-high heat. Fry the patties for about 6 minutes until golden brown on both sides, flipping once.

Remove from the heat to a plate lined with paper towels. Set aside.

Combine the remaining mayo and mustard in a small bowl. Stir well.

Serve the salmon cakes with the mayo dipping sauce on the side.

Nutrition

Calories: 382.9 Fat: 31.3g

Protein: 24.2g Carbs: 1.1g Fiber: 0g

Baked Salmon with Mayo Sauce

Preparation Time: 10 minutes
Cooking Time: 10 minutes
Servings: 2

Ingredients

Two tablespoons ghee, melted
2 (6-ounce) salmon fillets, skin on and patted dry
Pink Himalayan salt, to taste
Freshly ground black pepper, to taste

Mayo Sauce

¼ cup mayonnaise
One tablespoon Dijon mustard
Pinch garlic powder
Two tablespoons fresh dill, minced

Directions

Preheat the oven to 450°F (235°C). Generously grease a baking dish with melted ghee.

In a bowl, rub the salmon fillets with salt and pepper, then transfer to the greased baking dish.

Mix the mayo, mustard, garlic powder, and dill in a small bowl. Brush both sides of each fillet generously with the mayo mixture.

Bake in the preheated oven for about 7 to 9 minutes until cooked through.

Remove from the oven and serve on plates.

Nutrition

Calories: 512.9
Fat: 41.3g
Protein: 33.2g
Carbs: 2.1g
Fiber: 1g

Buttered Scallops with Herbs

Preparation Time: 10 minutes

Cooking Time: 10 minutes

Servings: 4

Ingredients

1 pound (454 g) sea scallops, cleaned and patted dry

Freshly ground black pepper, to taste

Eight tablespoons butter, divided

Two teaspoons minced garlic

Two teaspoons chopped fresh basil

One teaspoon chopped fresh thyme

Juice of 1 lemon

Directions

In a bowl, lightly season the sea scallops with black pepper.

Melt two tablespoons of butter in a large skillet over medium heat. Fry the scallops for about 2 to 3 minutes on each side or until golden brown.

Remove from the heat and set the sea scallops aside on a plate.

Melt the remaining butter in the same skillet and sauté the garlic for about 3 minutes until tender.

Add the sea scallops, basil, thyme, and lemon juice, and cook for 2 minutes more.

Remove from the heat and serve on plates.

Nutrition

Calories: 311.9

Fat: 24.3g

Protein: 19.2g

Carbs: 4.1g

Fiber: 0g

Lemony and Spicy Shrimp

Preparation Time: 10 minutes
Cooking Time: 15 minutes
Servings: 2

Ingredients

One lemon halved

Three tablespoons melted butter

½ pound (227 g) shrimp, peeled and deveined, with tail off

Two garlic cloves, crushed

Pink Himalayan salt and freshly ground black pepper, to taste

¼ teaspoon red pepper flakes

Directions

Preheat the oven to 425°F (220°C).

Cut one half of lemon into slices and cut another half of lemon into two wedges.

Put the melted butter on a baking dish, add the shrimp and garlic to the baking dish. Sprinkle the salt, black pepper, and red pepper flakes to season.

Add the lemon slices to the baking dish—Bake in the preheated oven for 15 minutes. Flip the shrimp halfway through the cooking time or until the shrimp is a little white.

Transfer the cooked shrimp to a large plate and squeeze the lemon wedges on top before serving.

Nutrition

Calories: 327.9

Fat: 20.3g

Protein: 32.2g

Carbs: 4.1g

Fiber: 1g

Fried Halibut with Citrus Sauce

Preparation Time: 10 minutes
Cooking Time: 15 minutes
Servings: 4

Ingredients

4 (5-ounce/142g) halibut fillets, each about 1 inch thick
Sea salt and freshly ground black pepper, to taste
¼ cup butter
Two teaspoons garlic, minced
One minced shallot
Two teaspoons fresh parsley, chopped
Two tablespoons olive oil

Citrus Sauce

One tablespoon freshly squeezed lemon juice
One tablespoon freshly squeezed lime juice
Three tablespoons dry white wine

Directions

On a clean work surface, pat the halibut fillets dry with paper towels. Rub both sides of each fillet with salt and pepper, then set them aside on a plate.

In a saucepan, melt the butter over medium heat. Add the garlic and shallots, and sauté for about 3 minutes until fragrant. Pour in the lemon juice, lime juice, and white wine while whisking. Bring the liquid to a simmer for 2 minutes until the citrus sauce is thickened.

Remove from the heat and scatter the parsley over the sauce. Set aside.

Heat the olive oil in a large skillet over medium-high heat. Add the seasoned fillets and fry for 5 minutes per side until lightly browned. Remove the fillets from the heat to four serving plates and drizzle each fillet with the citrus sauce. Serve warm.

Nutrition

Calories: 334.8 Fat: 26.4g
Protein: 22.2g Carbs: 2.1g Fiber: 0g

Fish curry with Kale and Cilantro

Preparation Time: 10 minutes

Cooking Time: 20 minutes

Servings: 4

Ingredients

Two tablespoons coconut oil

Two teaspoons garlic, minced

1½ tablespoons grated fresh ginger

½ teaspoon ground cumin

One tablespoon curry powder

2 cups of coconut milk

16 ounces (454 g) firm white fish, cut into 1-inch chunks

1 cup kale, shredded

Two tablespoons cilantro, chopped

Directions

In a large saucepan, melt the coconut oil over medium heat.

Add the garlic and ginger and sauté for about 2 minutes until tender.

Fold in the cumin and curry powder, then cook for 1 to 2 minutes until fragrant.

Add the coconut milk and bring it to a rapid boil. When it starts to boil, turn down the heat to low and simmer until the flavors mellow, about 5 minutes.

Add the fish chunks and simmer for 10 minutes until the fish flakes easily with a fork, stirring once.

Scatter the shredded kale and chopped cilantro over the fish, then cook for 2 minutes more until softened.

Allow cooling for 5 minutes before serving.

Nutrition

Calories: 402.9

Fat: 31.3g

Protein: 26.2g

Carbs: 4.1g

Fiber: 1g

Browned Salmon with Tomato Salad

Preparation Time: 15 minutes
Cooking Time: 15 minutes
Servings: 4

Ingredients

½ cup halved cherry tomatoes
One avocado, peeled, pitted, and diced
Juice of 1 lemon
Zest of 1 lemon
One scallion, white and green parts, chopped
½ teaspoon ground coriander
One teaspoon ground cumin
½ teaspoon onion powder
Pinch cayenne pepper
¼ teaspoon of sea salt
Pinch freshly ground black pepper
4 (4-ounce / 113-g) boneless, skinless salmon fillets
Two tablespoons olive oil

Directions

Make the salad: Mix the tomatoes, avocado, lemon juice, lemon zest, and scallion in a bowl. Stir to combine well and set aside.

Preheat the oven to 400°F (205°C) and line a baking sheet with aluminum foil. Set aside.

Combine the coriander, cumin, onion powder, cayenne, salt, and pepper in a separate bowl. Mix well.

Slather the fillets with the spice mixture, then transfer to the prepared baking sheet.

Pour the olive oil over each fillet and roast in the preheated oven for 15 minutes until just cooked through.

Remove the fish from the heat and serve alongside the tomato salad.

Nutrition

Calories: 329.9 Fat: 26.3g
Protein: 22.2g Carbs: 1.1g Fiber: 3g

Crispy Prosciutto-Wrapped Haddock Fillets

Preparation Time: 10 minutes
Cooking Time: 17 minutes
Servings: 4

Ingredients

4 (4-ounce/113g) haddock fillets, about 1 inch thick, patted dry

Sea salt and freshly ground black pepper, to taste

4 slices (2-ounce/57g) prosciutto

Three tablespoons olive oil

Juice and zest of 1 lemon

Directions

Preheat the oven to 350°F (180°C) and line a baking sheet with parchment paper. Set aside.

In a bowl, lightly season the haddock fillets with salt and pepper. Tightly wrap each fillet with a slice of prosciutto.

Arrange the prosciutto-wrapped fillets on the prepared baking sheet and drizzle with olive oil.

Bake in the preheated oven until cooked through, about 15 to 17 minutes.

Serve topped with the lemon juice and zest.

Nutrition

Calories: 285.9

Fat: 18.3g

Protein: 29.2g

Carbs: 1.1g

Fiber: 0g

Sodium: 76mg

Cheesy and Buttered Salmon

Preparation Time: 15 minutes

Cooking Time: 12 minutes

Servings: 5

Ingredients

Two tablespoons butter, at room temperature

½ cup Asiago cheese

Two teaspoons minced garlic

Two tablespoons freshly squeezed lemon juice

One teaspoon chopped fresh basil

One teaspoon chopped fresh oregano

4 (5-ounce/142g) salmon fillets, patted dry

One tablespoon olive oil

Directions

Preheat the oven to 350°F (180°C) and line a baking sheet with parchment paper. Set aside.

Make the topping: Combine the butter, Asiago cheese, garlic, lemon juice, basil, and oregano in a bowl. Toss well until completely mixed.

Arrange the salmon fillets, skin-side down, on the prepared baking sheet. Divide the topping among the fillets and spread it all over with the back of a spoon. Pour the olive oil over the fillets.

Bake in the preheated oven for about 12 minutes, or until the topping is golden brown and the fish flakes easily with a fork.

Remove from the oven and serve hot.

Nutrition

Calories: 359.9

Fat: 28.3g

Protein: 24.2g

Carbs: 2.1g

Fiber: 0g

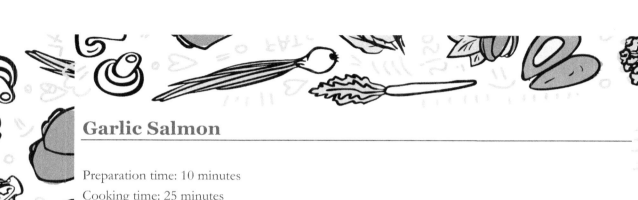

Garlic Salmon

Preparation time: 10 minutes
Cooking time: 25 minutes
Servings: 2

Ingredients

Two salmon fillets, skinless and boneless
Salt and pepper to the taste
Two tablespoons olive oil
Two garlic cloves, minced
One red chili, chopped
One small piece of ginger, grated
Juice of 1 lime
One tablespoon cilantro, chopped

Directions

In a roasting pan, combine the salmon with the oil, garlic, and the rest of the ingredients except the cilantro, toss, introduce in the oven at 350 degrees F and bake for 25 minutes.

Divide everything between plates and serve with the cilantro sprinkled on top.

Nutrition

Calories: 251
Fat: 15.9
Fiber: 5.9
Carbs: 26.4
Protein: 12.4

Salmon and Creamy Endives

Preparation time: 10 minutes

Cooking time: 15 minutes

Servings: 4

Ingredients

Four salmon fillets, boneless

Two endives, shredded

Juice of 1 lime

Salt and black pepper to the taste

¼ cup chicken stock

1 cup Greek yogurt

¼ cup green olives pitted and chopped

¼ cup fresh chives, chopped

Three tablespoons olive oil

Directions

Heat a pan with half of the oil over medium heat, add the endives and the rest of the ingredients except the chives and the salmon, toss, cook for 6 minutes, and divide between plates.

Heat another pan with the rest of the oil, add the salmon, season with salt and pepper, cook for 4 minutes on each side, add next to the creamy endives mix, sprinkle the chives on top, and serve.

Nutrition

Calories: 266

Fat: 13.9

Fiber: 11.1

Carbs: 23.8

Protein: 17.5

Parsley Trout and Capers

Preparation time: 10 minutes

Cooking time: 10 minutes

Servings: 4

Ingredients

Four trout fillets, boneless

3 ounces tomato sauce

Handful parsley, chopped

Two tablespoons olive oil

Salt and black pepper to the taste

Directions

Heat a pan with the oil over medium-high heat, add the fish, salt, and pepper and cook for 3 minutes on each side.

Add the rest of the ingredients, cook everything for 4 minutes more.

Divide everything between plates and serve.

Nutrition

Calories: 308

Fat: 17

Fiber: 1

Carbs: 3

Protein: 16

Baked Trout and Fennel

Preparation time: 10 minutes
Cooking time: 22 minutes
Servings: 4

Ingredients

One fennel bulb, sliced
Two tablespoons olive oil
One yellow onion, sliced
Three teaspoons Italian seasoning
Four rainbow trout fillets, boneless
¼ cup panko breadcrumbs
½ cup kalamata olives pitted and halved
Juice of 1 lemon

Directions

Spread the fennel, the onion, and the rest of the ingredients except the trout and the breadcrumbs on a baking sheet lined with parchment paper, toss them and cook at 400 degrees F for 10 minutes.

Add the fish dredged in breadcrumbs and seasoned with salt and pepper and cook it at 400 degrees F for 6 minutes on each side.

Divide the mix between plates and serve.

Nutrition

Calories: 306
Fat: 8.9
Fiber: 11.1
Carbs: 23.8
Protein: 14.5

CHAPTER 17:

APPETIZERS AND SIDES

Spiced Jalapeno Bites with Tomato

Preparation Time: 10 minutes
Cooking Time: 0 minutes
Servings: 4

Ingredients

1 cup turkey ham, chopped
1/4 jalapeño pepper, minced
1/4 cup mayonnaise
1/3 tablespoon Dijon mustard four tomatoes, sliced
Salt and black pepper, to taste
One tablespoon parsley, chopped

Directions

In a bowl, mix the turkey ham, jalapeño pepper, mayo, mustard, salt, and pepper.

Spread out the tomato slices on four serving plates, then top each plate with a spoonful of turkey ham mixture.

Serve garnished with chopped parsley.

Nutrition

Calories: 250
Fat: 14.1g
Fiber: 3.7g
Carbs: 4.1g
Protein: 18.9g

Coconut Crab Cakes

Preparation Time: 20 minutes
Cooking Time: 25 minutes
Servings: 4

Ingredients

One tablespoon of minced garlic
Two pasteurized eggs
Two teaspoons of coconut oil
3/4 cup of coconut flakes
3/4 cup chopped spinach
1/4 pound crabmeat
1/4 cup of chopped leek
1/2 cup extra virgin olive oil
1/2 teaspoon of pepper
1/4 onion diced
Salt

Directions

Pour the crabmeat into a bowl, then add in the coconut flakes and mix well.

Whisk eggs in a bowl, then mix in leek and spinach.

Season the egg mixture with pepper, two pinches of salt, and garlic.

Then, pour the eggs into the crab and stir well.

Preheat a pan, heat extra virgin olive, and fry the crab evenly from each side until golden brown. Remove from pan and serve hot.

Nutrition

Calories: 254
Fat: 9.5g
Fiber: 5.4g
Carbs:4.1g
Protein: 8.9g

Tuna Cakes

Preparation Time: 15 minutes
Cooking Time: 10 minutes
Servings: 2

Ingredients

1 (15-ounce) can water-packed tuna, drained
1/2 celery stalk, chopped
Two tablespoons fresh parsley, chopped
One teaspoon fresh dill, chopped
Two tablespoons walnuts, chopped
Two tablespoons mayonnaise
One organic egg, beaten
One tablespoon butter
3 cups lettuce

Directions

For burgers: Add all ingredients (except the butter and lettuce) to a bowl and mix until well combined.
Make two equal-sized patties from the mixture.
Melt some butter and cook the patties for about 2–3 minutes.
Carefully flip the side and cook for about 2–3 minutes.
Divide the lettuce onto serving plates.
Top each plate with one burger and serve.

Nutrition

Calories: 267
Fat: 12.5g
Fiber: 9.4g
Carbs:3.8g
Protein: 11.5g

Creamed Spinach

Preparation Time: 10 minutes
Cooking Time: 15 minutes
Servings: 4

Ingredients

Two tablespoons unsalted butter
One small yellow onion, chopped
1 cup cream cheese, softened
2 (10-ounce) packages frozen spinach, thawed and squeezed dry
2–3 tablespoons water
Salt and ground black pepper, as required
One teaspoon fresh lemon juice

Directions

Melt some butter and sauté the onion for about 6–8 minutes.
Add the cream cheese and cook for about 2 minutes or until melted completely.
Stir in the water and spinach and cook for about 4–5 minutes.
Stir in the salt, black pepper, and lemon juice, and remove from heat.
Serve immediately.

Nutrition

Calories: 214
Fat: 9.5g
Fiber: 2.3g
Carbs: 2.1g
Protein: 4.2g

Tempura Zucchini with Cream Cheese Dip

Preparation Time: 15 minutes
Cooking Time: 15 minutes
Servings: 4

Ingredients

1 1/2 cups (200 g) almond flour
2 tbsp. heavy cream
1 tsp. salt
2 tbsp. olive oil + extra for frying
1 1/4 cups (300 ml) water
1/2 tbsp. sugar-free maple syrup
Two large zucchinis, cut into 1-inch-thick strips

Cream Cheese Dip

8 oz cream cheese, room temperature
1/2 cup (113 g) sour cream
1 tsp. taco seasoning
One scallion, chopped
One green chili, deseeded and minced

Directions

In a bowl, mix the almond flour, heavy cream, salt, peanut oil, water, and maple syrup.

Dredge the zucchini strips in the mixture until well-coated.

Heat about four tablespoons of olive oil in a non-stick skillet.

Working in batches, use tongs to remove the zucchinis (draining extra liquid) into the oil.

Fry per side for 1 to 2 minutes and remove the zucchinis onto a paper towel-lined plate to drain grease. In a bowl or container, the cream cheese, taco seasoning, sour cream, scallion, and green chili must be mixed, Serve the tempura zucchinis with the cream cheese dip.

Nutrition

Calories: 316 Fat: 8.4g
Fiber: 9.3g Carbs: 4.1g Protein: 5.1g

Bacon and Feta Skewers

Preparation Time: 15 minutes

Cooking Time: 10 minutes

Servings: 4

Ingredients

2 lb. feta cheese, cut into eight cubes

Eight bacon slices

Four bamboo skewers, soaked

One zucchini, cut into eight bite-size cubes

Salt and black pepper to taste

3 tbsp. almond oil for brushing

Directions

Wrap each feta cube with a bacon slice.

Thread one wrapped feta on a skewer; add a zucchini cube, then another wrapped feta, and another zucchini.

Repeat the threading process with the remaining skewers.

Preheat a grill pan to medium heat, generously brush with the avocado oil and grill the skewer on both sides for 3 to 4 minutes per side or until the set is golden brown and the bacon cooked.

Serve afterward with the tomato salsa.

Nutrition

Calories: 290

Fat: 15.1g

Fiber: 4.2g

Carbs: 4.1g

Protein: 11.8g

Avocado and Prosciutto Deviled Eggs

Preparation Time: 20 minutes
Cooking Time: 10 minutes
Servings: 4

Ingredients

Four eggs
Ice bath
Four prosciutto slices, chopped
One avocado pitted and peeled
1 tbsp. mustard - 1 tsp. plain vinegar
1 tbsp. heavy cream
1 tbsp. chopped fresh cilantro
Salt and black pepper to taste
1/2 cup (113 g) mayonnaise
1 tbsp. coconut cream - 1/4 tsp. cayenne pepper
1 tbsp. avocado oil
1 tbsp. chopped fresh parsley

Directions

Boil the eggs for 8 minutes.

Empty the eggs into the ice bath, sit for 3 minutes, and then peel the eggs. Slice the eggs lengthwise into halves and empty the egg yolks into a bowl. Arrange the egg whites on a plate with the hole side facing upwards. While the eggs are cooked, heat a non-stick skillet over medium heat and cook the prosciutto for 5 to 8 minutes. Remove the prosciutto onto a paper towel-lined plate to drain grease.

Put the avocado slices into the egg yolks and mash both ingredients with a fork until smooth. Mix in the mustard, vinegar, heavy cream, cilantro, salt, and black pepper until well-blended. Spoon the mixture into a piping bag and press the mixture into the egg holes until well-filled.

In a bowl, whisk the mayonnaise, coconut cream, cayenne pepper, and avocado oil. On serving plates, spoon some of the mayonnaise sauce and slightly smear it in a circular movement. Top with the deviled eggs, scatter the prosciutto on top, and garnish with the parsley. Enjoy immediately.

Nutrition

Calories: 265 Fat: 11.7g Fiber: 4.1g Carbs: 3.1 g Protein: 7.9 g

Chili-Lime Tuna Salad

Preparation Time: 10 minutes
Cooking Time: 0 minutes
Servings: 2

Ingredients

One tablespoon of lime juice
1/3 cup of mayonnaise
1/4 teaspoon of salt
One teaspoon of Tajin chili lime seasoning
1/8 teaspoon of pepper
One medium stalk of celery (finely chopped)
2 cups of romaine lettuce (chopped roughly)
Two tablespoons of red onion (finely chopped)
optional: chopped green onion, black pepper, lemon juice
5 oz canned tuna

Directions

Using a bowl of medium size, mix some of the ingredients such as lime, pepper, and chili-lime
Then, add tuna and vegetables to the pot and stir. You can serve with cucumber, celery, or a bed of greens

Nutrition

Calories: 259
Fat: 11.3g
Fiber: 7.4g
Carbs: 2.9g
Protein: 12.9g

Parmesan Eggplant Bites

Preparation Time: 10 minutes
Cooking Time: 30 minutes
Servings: 8

Ingredients

Two eggs, beaten
3 oz Parmesan, grated
One tablespoon coconut flakes
½ teaspoon ground paprika
One teaspoon salt
Two eggplants, trimmed

Directions

Slice the eggplants into thin circles. Use the vegetable slicer for this step.

After this, sprinkle the vegetables with the salt and mix. Leave them for 5-10 minutes.

Then drain eggplant juice and sprinkle them with ground paprika.

Mix up together coconut flakes and Parmesan.

Dip every eggplant circle in the egg and then coat it in Parmesan mixture.

Line the baking tray with parchment and place eggplants on it.

Bake the vegetables for 30 minutes at 360F. Flip the eggplants into another side after 12 minutes of cooking.

Nutrition

Calories: 87
Fat: 3.9g
Fiber: 5g
Carbs: 8.7g
Protein: 6.2g

Crab-stuffed Avocado

Preparation Time: 20 minutes

Cooking Time: 0 minutes

Servings: 2

Ingredients

One avocado

1/2 teaspoon lemon

4 1/2 ounces Dungeness crabmeat

1/2 cup cream cheese

1/4 cup red bell pepper

1/4 cup cucumber

1/2 scallion,

One teaspoon cilantro

Pinch sea salt

Freshly ground black pepper

Directions

Brush the cut edges of the avocado with the lemon juice and set the halves aside on a plate.

The crabmeat, cream cheese, red pepper, cucumber, scallion, cilantro, salt, and pepper must be well mixed in a bowl or container.

The crab mixture will then be divided between the avocado

Nutrition

Calories: 239

Fat: 11.4g

Fiber: 8.1g

Carbs: 3.8g

Protein: 5.9g

Grilled Halloumi Cheese with Eggs

Preparation Time: 15 minutes

Cooking Time:10 minutes

Servings: 4

Ingredients

Four slices of halloumi cheese

3 tsp. olive oil

1 tsp. the dried Greek seasoning blend

1 tbsp. olive oil

Six eggs, beaten

1/2 tsp. sea salt

1/4 tsp. crushed red pepper flakes

1 1/2 cups avocado, pitted and sliced

1 cup grape tomatoes, halved

4 tbsp. pecans, chopped

Directions

Preheat your grill to medium.

Set the Halloumi in the center of a piece of heavy-duty foil.

Sprinkle oil over the Halloumi and apply a Greek seasoning blend.

Close the foil to create a packet.

Grill for about 15 minutes, then slices into four pieces.

In a frying pan, warm one tablespoon of oil and cook the eggs.

Stir well to create large and soft curds—season with salt and pepper.

Put the eggs and grilled cheese in a serving bowl.

Serve alongside tomatoes and avocado, decorated with chopped pecans.

Nutrition

Calories: 219 Fat: 5.1g

Fiber: 4.9g Carbs: 1.5 g Protein: 3.9g

Creamy Kale Salad

Preparation Time: 15 minutes
Cooking Time: 0 minutes
Servings: 3

Ingredients

One bunch spinach
1 1/2 tablespoon lemon juice
1 cup sour cream
1 cup roasted macadamia
Two tablespoons sesame seeds oil
1 1/2 garlic clove, minced
1/2 teaspoon black pepper
1/4 teaspoon salt
Two tablespoons lime juice
One bunch kale
1 1/2 Avocado, diced
1/4 cup Pecans, chopped

Directions

First of all, please confirm you've all the ingredients out there. Chop kale and wash kale, then remove the ribs.

Now transfer kale to a large bowl.

One thing remains to be done. Add sour cream, lime juice, macadamia, sesame seeds oil, pepper, salt, garlic.

Finally, mix thoroughly. Top with your avocado and pecans. Serve& enjoy.

Nutrition

Calories: 291
Fat: 5.1g
Fiber: 12.9g
Carbs: 4.3g
Protein: 11.8g

Quinoa Salad with Fresh Mint and Parsley

Preparation Time: 10 minutes

Cooking Time: 15 minutes

Servings: 4

Ingredients

2 cups of quinoa

1/2 cup of almond nut

Three tablespoons of fresh parsley (chopped)

1/2 cup of chopped green onions

Three tablespoons of chopped fresh mint

Three tablespoons of olive oil

Two tablespoons of lemon juice

One teaspoon of garlic salt

1/2 teaspoon of salt and pepper

Directions

Place a saucepan on high heat.

Add the quinoa and water and just let it boil for around 15 minutes, then reduce the heat and drain.

Pour the drained quinoa into a large bowl, add the parsley, almond nuts, and mint.

In a bowl or container, add the olive oil, garlic salt, and lemon juice together.

Whisk the mixture well until it's well combined and pour over the quinoa.

Combine the mixture well until everything is well dispersed.

Add the salt and black pepper to taste.

Place the quinoa mixture bowl in the refrigerator.

Nutrition

Calories: 241

Fat: 8.4g

Fiber: 11.4g

Carbs:2.1 g

Protein: 9.3g

Cucumber Sola Sandwich Bites

Preparation Time: 5 minutes
Cooking Time: 0 minutes
Servings: 2

Ingredients

One cucumber, sliced
4 slices sola bread
Two tablespoons cream cheese, soft
One tablespoon chives, chopped
¼ cup avocado, peeled, pitted, and mashed
One teaspoon mustard
Salt and black pepper to the taste

Directions

Spread the mashed avocado on each bread slice, also spread the rest of the ingredients except the cucumber slices.

Divide the cucumber slices into the bread slices, cut each slice in thirds, arrange on a platter, and serve as an appetizer.

Nutrition

Calories: 187
Fat: 12.4g
Fiber: 2.1g
Carbs: 4.5g
Protein: 8.2g

Tomato Bruschetta

Preparation Time: 10 minutes

Cooking Time: 10 minutes

Servings: 6

Ingredients

One baguette, sliced

1/3 cup basil, chopped

Six tomatoes, cubed

Two garlic cloves, minced

A pinch of salt and black pepper

One teaspoon olive oil

One tablespoon balsamic vinegar

½ teaspoon garlic powder

Cooking spray

Directions

Place the baguette slices on a baking sheet lined with parchment paper, grease with cooking spray. Cook it at 400 degrees for 10 minutes.

Combine the tomatoes with the basil and the remaining ingredients, toss well and leave aside for 10 minutes. Divide the tomato mix on each baguette slice, arrange them all on a platter and serve.

Nutrition

Calories: 162

Fat: 4g

Fiber: 7g

Carbs: 29g

Protein: 4g

CHAPTER 18:

VEGETABLES

Celery Salad

Preparation Time: 10 minutes
Cooking Time: 10 minutes
Servings: 8

Ingredients

5 cups celery, cubed
1/4 cup fresh parsley, chopped
1/4 tsp red pepper flakes
1 tbsp olive oil
1/3 cup mayonnaise
1/2 tbsp oregano
2 tbsp capers
3/4 cup feta cheese, crumbled
1 cup olives, halved
3 cups of water
3/4 cup onion, chopped
Pepper
Salt

Directions

Add celery, onion, and salt into the instant pot.
Seal pot with lid and cook on high for 3 minutes.
Once done, release pressure using quick release. Remove lid.
Remove potatoes from the pot and place in a large mixing bowl.
Add remaining ingredients and stir everything well.
Serve and enjoy.

Nutrition

Calories: 152 Fat: 9.9g
Carbs: 13.6g Sugar: 2.1g Protein: 3.5g Cholesterol: 15mg

Fried Eggplant Rolls

Preparation Time: 20 minutes
Cooking Time: 10 minutes
Servings: 6

Ingredients

Two large eggplants, trimmed and cut lengthwise into ¼-inch-thick slices

One teaspoon salt

1 cup shredded ricotta cheese

4 ounces (113 g) goat cheese, shredded

¼ cup finely chopped fresh basil

½ teaspoon freshly ground black pepper

Olive oil spray

Directions

Add the eggplant slices to a colander and season with salt. Set aside for 15 to 20 minutes.

Mix the ricotta and goat cheese, basil, and black pepper in a large bowl and stir to combine. Set aside. Dry the eggplant slices with paper towels and lightly mist them with olive oil spray.

Heat a large skillet over medium heat and lightly spray it with olive oil spray. Arrange the eggplant slices in the skillet and fry each side for 3 minutes until golden brown.

Remove from the heat to a paper towel-lined plate and rest for 5 minutes. Make the eggplant rolls: Lay the eggplant slices on a flat work surface and top each slice with a prepared cheese mixture tablespoon. Roll them up and serve immediately.

Nutrition

Calories: 254
Fat: 14.9g
Protein: 15.3g
Fiber: 7.1g
Carbs: 15g

Roasted Veggies and Brown Rice Bowl

Preparation Time: 15 minutes
Cooking Time: 20 minutes
Servings: 4

Ingredients

2 cups cauliflower florets

2 cups broccoli florets

1 (15-ounces/425-g) can chickpeas, drained and rinsed

1 cup carrot slices (about 1-inch thick)

2 to 3 tablespoons extra-virgin olive oil, divided

Salt and freshly ground black pepper, to taste

Nonstick cooking spray - 2 cups cooked brown rice

2 to 3 tablespoons sesame seeds, for garnish

Dressing

3 to 4 tablespoons tahini

Two tablespoons honey

One lemon, juiced - One garlic clove, minced

Salt and freshly ground black pepper, to taste

Directions

Preheat the oven to 400ºF (205ºC). Spritz two baking sheets with nonstick cooking spray.

Spread the cauliflower and broccoli on the first baking sheet and the second with the chickpeas and carrot slices. Drizzle each sheet with half of the olive oil and sprinkle with salt and pepper. Toss to coat well. Roast the chickpeas and carrot slices in the preheated oven for 10 minutes, leaving the carrots tender but crisp, and the cauliflower and broccoli for 20 minutes until fork tender. Stir them once halfway through the cooking time. Meanwhile, make the dressing: Whisk together the tahini, honey, lemon juice, garlic, salt, and pepper in a small bowl.

Divide the cooked brown rice among four bowls. Top each bowl evenly with roasted vegetables and dressing. Sprinkle the sesame seeds on top for garnish before serving.

Nutrition

Calories: 453 Fat: 17.8g Protein: 12.1g Fiber: 11.2g Carbs: 12g

Cauliflower Hash with Carrots

Preparation Time: 10 minutes

Cooking Time: 10 minutes

Servings: 4

Ingredients

Three tablespoons extra-virgin olive oil

One large onion, chopped

One tablespoon minced garlic

2 cups diced carrots

4 cups cauliflower florets

½ teaspoon ground cumin

One teaspoon salt

Directions

In a large skillet, heat the olive oil over medium heat.

Add the onion and garlic and sauté for 1 minute. Stir in the carrots and stir-fry for 3 minutes. Add the cauliflower florets, cumin, and salt and toss to combine.

Cover and cook for 3 minutes until lightly browned. Stir well and cook, uncovered, for 3 to 4 minutes, until softened. Remove from the heat and serve warm.

Nutrition

Calories: 158

Fat: 10.8g

Protein: 3.1g

Fiber: 5.1g

Carbs: 10g

Garlicky Zucchini Cubes with Mint

Preparation Time: 5 minutes
Cooking Time: 10 minutes
Servings: 4

Ingredients
Three large green zucchinis
Three tablespoons extra-virgin olive oil
One large onion, chopped
Three cloves garlic, minced
One teaspoon salt
One teaspoon dried mint

Directions
Heat the olive oil in a large skillet over medium heat.
Add the onion and garlic and sauté for 3 minutes, stirring constantly, or until softened.
Stir in the zucchini cubes and salt and cook for 5 minutes, or until the zucchini is browned and tender.
Add the mint to the skillet and toss to combine, then continue cooking for 2 minutes.
Serve warm.

Nutrition
Calories: 146
Fat: 10.6g
Protein: 4.2g
Fiber: 3g
Carbs: 5.5g

Zucchini and Artichokes Bowl with Faro

Preparation Time: 15 minutes

Cooking Time: 10 minutes

Servings: 4

Ingredients

1/3 cup extra-virgin olive oil

1/3 cup chopped red onions

½ cup chopped red bell pepper

Two garlic cloves, minced

1 cup zucchini, cut into ½-inch-thick slices

½ cup coarsely chopped artichokes

½ cup canned chickpeas drained and rinsed

3 cups cooked faro

Salt and freshly ground black pepper, to taste

½ cup crumbled feta cheese, for serving (optional)

¼ cup sliced olives, for serving (optional)

Two tablespoons fresh basil, chiffonade, for serving (optional)

Three tablespoons balsamic vinegar, for serving (optional)

Directions

Heat the olive oil in a large skillet over medium heat until it shimmers. Add the onions, bell pepper, and garlic and sauté for 5 minutes, occasionally stirring, until softened.

Stir in the zucchini slices, artichokes, and chickpeas and sauté for about 5 minutes until slightly tender. Add the cooked faro and toss to combine until heated through. Sprinkle the salt and pepper to season.

Divide the mixture into bowls. Top each bowl evenly with feta cheese, olive slices, and basil and sprinkle with the balsamic vinegar, if desired.

Nutrition

Calories: 366 Fat: 19.9g

Carbs: 10.1g Protein: 9.3g Fiber: 9g

Five-Filling Zucchini Fritters

Preparation Time: 15 minutes
Cooking Time: 5 minutes
Servings: 14

Ingredients

4 cups grated zucchini
Salt, to taste
Two large eggs, lightly beaten
1/3 cup sliced scallions (green and white parts)
2/3 all-purpose flour
1/8 teaspoon black pepper
Two tablespoons olive oil

Directions

Put the grated zucchini in a colander and lightly season with salt. Set aside to rest for 10 minutes. Squeeze out as much liquid from the grated zucchini as possible.

Pour the grated zucchini into a bowl. Fold in the beaten eggs, scallions, flour, salt, and pepper, and stir until everything is well combined.

Heat the olive oil in a large skillet over medium heat until hot.

Drop three tablespoons mounds of the zucchini mixture onto the hot skillet to make each patty, pressing them lightly into rounds and spacing them about 2 inches apart.

Cook for 2 to 3 minutes. Flip the zucchini fritters and cook for 2 minutes more, or until they are golden brown and cooked through.

Remove from the heat to a plate lined with paper towels. Repeat with the remaining zucchini mixture. Serve hot.

Nutrition

Calories: 113
Carbs: 12g
Fat: 6.1g
Protein: 4g
Fiber: 1g

Moroccan Tagine with Vegetables

Preparation Time: 20 minutes

Cooking Time: 40 minutes

Servings: 2

Ingredients

Two tablespoons olive oil

½ onion, diced

One garlic clove, minced

2 cups cauliflower florets

One medium carrot, cut into 1-inch pieces

1 cup diced eggplant   .

1 (28-ounces/794-g) can whole tomatoes with their juices

1 (15-ounces/425-g) can chickpeas

Two small red potatoes

1 cup of water - ½ teaspoon cinnamon

½ teaspoon turmeric

One teaspoon cumin - ½ teaspoon salt

1 to 2 teaspoons harissa paste

Directions

In a Dutch oven, heat the olive oil over medium-high heat. Sauté the onion for 5 minutes, stirring occasionally, or until the onion is translucent.

Stir in the garlic, cauliflower florets, carrot, eggplant, tomatoes, and potatoes. I am using a wooden spoon or spatula to break up the tomatoes into smaller pieces.

Add the chickpeas, water, cinnamon, turmeric, cumin, and salt and stir to incorporate. Bring the mixture to a boil. Once it starts to boil, reduce the heat to medium-low. Stir in the harissa paste, cover, allow to simmer for about 40 minutes, or until the vegetables are softened. Taste and adjust seasoning as needed. Let the mixture cool for 5 minutes before serving.

Nutrition

Calories: 293 Carbs: 10g

Fat: 9.9g Protein: 11.2g Fiber: 12.1g

Chickpea Lettuce Wraps with Celery

Preparation Time: 10 minutes

Cooking Time: 0 minutes

Servings: 4

Ingredients

1 (15-ounces / 425-g) can low-sodium chickpeas

One celery stalk, thinly sliced

Two tablespoons finely chopped red onion

Two tablespoons unsalted tahini

Three tablespoons honey mustard

One tablespoon capers, undrained

12 butter lettuce leaves

Directions

In a bowl, mash the chickpeas with a potato masher or the back of a fork until mostly smooth. Add the celery, red onion, tahini, honey mustard, and capers to the bowl and stir until well incorporated.

For each serving, place three overlapping lettuce leaves on a plate and top with ¼ of the mashed chickpea filling, then roll up. Repeat with the remaining lettuce leaves and chickpea mixture.

Nutrition

Calories: 182

Fat: 7.1g

Protein: 10.3g

Carbs: 9.2g

Fiber: 3g

Grilled Vegetable Skewers

Preparation Time: 15 minutes

Cooking Time: 10 minutes

Servings: 4

Ingredients

Four medium red onions, peeled and sliced into six wedges

Four medium zucchinis, cut into 1-inch-thick slices

Two beefsteak tomatoes, cut into quarters

Four red bell peppers, cut into 2-inch squares

Two orange bell peppers, cut into 2-inch squares

Two yellow bell peppers, cut into 2-inch squares

Two tablespoons plus one teaspoon olive oil, divided

Directions

Preheat the grill to medium-high heat. Skewer the vegetables by alternating between red onion, zucchini, tomatoes, and the different colored bell peppers. Brush them with two tablespoons of olive oil.

Oil the grill grates with one teaspoon of olive oil and grill the vegetable skewers for 5 minutes. Flip the skewers and grill for 5 minutes more, or until they are cooked to your liking. Let the skewers cool for 5 minutes before serving.

Nutrition

Calories: 115

Fat: 3g

Carbs: 4.5g

Protein: 3.5g

Fiber: 4.7g

Stuffed Portobello Mushroom with Tomatoes

Preparation Time: 10 minutes

Cooking Time: 15 minutes

Servings: 4

Ingredients

Four large portobello mushroom caps

Three tablespoons extra-virgin olive oil

Salt and freshly ground black pepper, to taste

Four sun-dried tomatoes

1 cup shredded mozzarella cheese, divided

½ to ¾ cup low-sodium tomato sauce

Directions

Preheat the broiler on high. Arrange the mushroom caps on a baking sheet and drizzle with olive oil. Sprinkle with salt and pepper. Broil for 1o minutes, flipping the mushroom caps halfway through until browned on the top.

Remove from the broil. Spoon one tomato, two tablespoons of cheese, and 2 to 3 tablespoons of sauce onto each mushroom cap. Return the mushroom caps to the broiler and continue broiling for 2 to 3 minutes. Cool for 5 minutes before serving.

Nutrition

Calories: 217

Fat: 15.8g

Protein: 11.2g

Carbs: 10.4g

Fiber: 2g

Wilted Dandelion Greens with Sweet Onion

Preparation Time: 15 minutes
Cooking Time: 15 minutes
Servings: 4

Ingredients

One tablespoon extra-virgin olive oil
Two garlic cloves, minced
1 Vidalia onion, thinly sliced
½ cup low-sodium vegetable broth
Two bunches of dandelion greens, roughly chopped
Freshly ground black pepper, to taste

Directions

Heat the olive oil in a large skillet over low heat. Add the garlic and onion and cook for 2 to 3 minutes, stirring occasionally, or until the onion is translucent.

Fold in the vegetable broth and dandelion greens and cook for 5 to 7 minutes until wilted, stirring frequently. Sprinkle with the black pepper and serve on a plate while warm.

Nutrition

Calories: 81
Carbs: 3g
Fat: 3.9g
Protein: 3.2g
Fiber: 4g

Celery and Mustard Greens

Preparation Time: 10 minutes

Cooking Time: 15 minutes

Servings: 4

Ingredients

½ cup low-sodium vegetable broth

One celery stalk, roughly chopped

½ sweet onion, chopped

½ large red bell pepper, thinly sliced

Two garlic cloves, minced

One bunch mustard greens, roughly chopped

Directions

Pour the vegetable broth into a large cast-iron pan and bring it to a simmer over medium heat. Stir in the celery, onion, bell pepper, and garlic. Cook uncovered for about 3 to 5 minutes, or until the onion is softened.

Add the mustard greens to the pan and stir well. Cover, reduce the heat to low, cook for an additional 10 minutes, or until the liquid is evaporated and the greens are wilted. Remove from the heat and serve warm.

Nutrition

Calories: 39

Protein: 3.1g

Carbs: 6.8g

Fiber: 3g

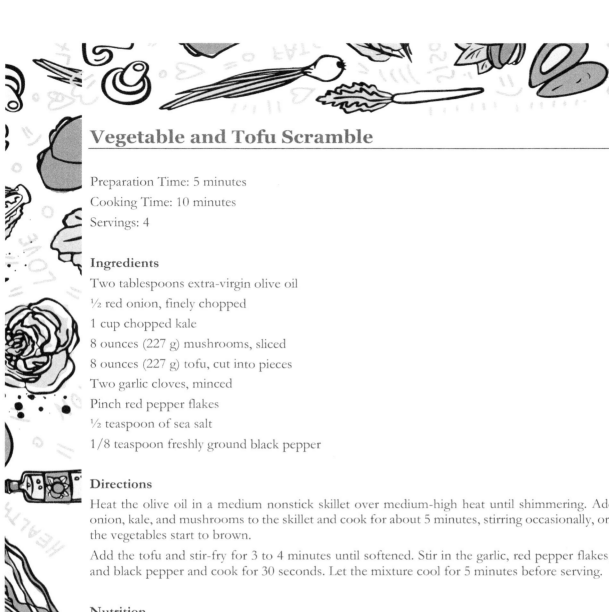

Vegetable and Tofu Scramble

Preparation Time: 5 minutes

Cooking Time: 10 minutes

Servings: 4

Ingredients

Two tablespoons extra-virgin olive oil

½ red onion, finely chopped

1 cup chopped kale

8 ounces (227 g) mushrooms, sliced

8 ounces (227 g) tofu, cut into pieces

Two garlic cloves, minced

Pinch red pepper flakes

½ teaspoon of sea salt

1/8 teaspoon freshly ground black pepper

Directions

Heat the olive oil in a medium nonstick skillet over medium-high heat until shimmering. Add the onion, kale, and mushrooms to the skillet and cook for about 5 minutes, stirring occasionally, or until the vegetables start to brown.

Add the tofu and stir-fry for 3 to 4 minutes until softened. Stir in the garlic, red pepper flakes, salt, and black pepper and cook for 30 seconds. Let the mixture cool for 5 minutes before serving.

Nutrition

Calories: 233

Fat: 15.9g

Carbs: 15g

Protein: 13.4g

Fiber: 2g

Simple Zoodles

Preparation Time: 10 minutes
Cooking Time: 5 minutes
Servings: 2

Ingredients

Two tablespoons avocado oil
Two medium zucchinis, spiralized
¼ teaspoon salt
Freshly ground black pepper, to taste

Directions

Heat the avocado oil in a large skillet over medium heat until it shimmers. Add the zucchini noodles, salt, and black pepper to the skillet and toss to coat. Cook for 1 to 2 minutes, constantly stirring, until tender. Serve warm.

Nutrition

Calories: 128
Fat: 14g
Protein: 0.3g
Carbs: 0.3g

CHAPTER 19:

DESSERT

Blueberry Frozen Yogurt

Preparation Time: 15 minutes

Cooking Time: 30 minutes

Servings: 4

Ingredients

1-pint blueberries, fresh

One small lemon, juiced and zested

2 cups yogurt, chilled

Directions

In a saucepan, combine the blueberries, lemon juice, and zest.

Heat over medium heat and allow to simmer for 15 minutes while stirring constantly.

Once the liquid has reduced, transfer the fruits to a bowl and cool in the fridge for another 15 minutes.

Once chilled, mix with the chilled yogurt.

Nutrition

Calories per serving: 233

Carbs: 52.2g

Protein: 3.5g

Fat: 2.9g

Cocoa Nut Spread

Preparation Time: 10 minutes
Cooking Time: 10 minutes
Servings: 4

Ingredients
1/4 cup unsweetened cocoa powder
1/4 tsp nutmeg
1 tsp vanilla
1/4 cup coconut oil
1 tsp liquid stevia
1/4 cup coconut cream
3 tbsp walnuts
1 cup almonds

Directions
Add walnut and almonds into the food processor and process until smooth.

Add oil and process for 1 minute. Transfer to the bowl and stir in vanilla, nutmeg, and liquid stevia.

Add coconut cream into the instant pot and set the pot on sauté mode.

Add almond mixture and cocoa powder and stir well and cook for 5 minutes.

Pour into the container and store it in the refrigerator for 30 minutes.

Serve and enjoy.

Nutrition
Calories: 342
Fat: 33.3g
Carbs: 9.6g
Sugar: 1.8g
Protein: 7.8g
Cholesterol: 0mg

Berry Nut Bowl

Preparation Time: 10 minutes
Cooking Time: 10 minutes
Servings: 2

Ingredients

1/4 cup pecans, chopped
1/4 cup shredded coconut
1 cup of water
3 tbsp coconut oil
1/2 tsp cinnamon
1 cup blueberries
1 cup raspberries
2 tbsp swerve

Directions

In a heat-safe dish, add coconut, coconut oil, blueberries, raspberries, and swerve and mix well.
Pour water into the instant pot, then place the trivet in the pot.
Place dish on top of the trivet.
Seal pot with lid and cook on high for 10 minutes.
Once done, release pressure using quick release. Remove lid.
Remove dish from pot carefully. Top with pecans and serve.

Nutrition

Calories: 338
Fat: 25.4g
Carbs: 47.2g
Sugar: 37.6g
Protein: 1.4g
Cholesterol 0mg

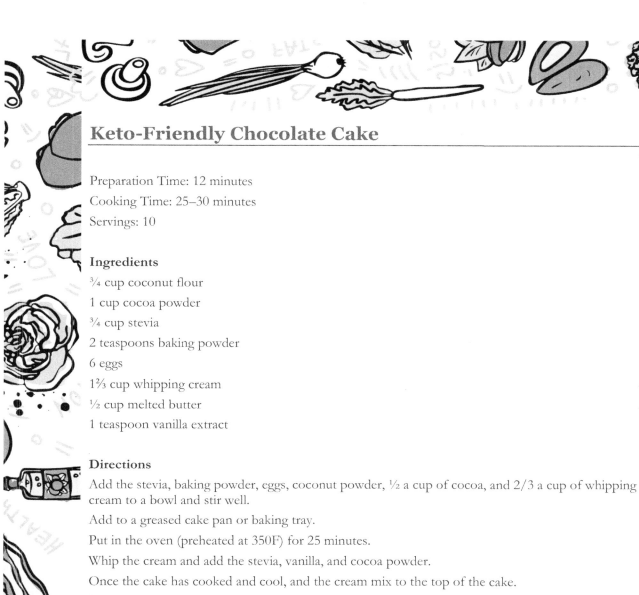

Keto-Friendly Chocolate Cake

Preparation Time: 12 minutes

Cooking Time: 25–30 minutes

Servings: 10

Ingredients

¾ cup coconut flour

1 cup cocoa powder

¾ cup stevia

2 teaspoons baking powder

6 eggs

1⅔ cup whipping cream

½ cup melted butter

1 teaspoon vanilla extract

Directions

Add the stevia, baking powder, eggs, coconut powder, ½ a cup of cocoa, and 2/3 a cup of whipping cream to a bowl and stir well.

Add to a greased cake pan or baking tray.

Put in the oven (preheated at 350F) for 25 minutes.

Whip the cream and add the stevia, vanilla, and cocoa powder.

Once the cake has cooked and cool, and the cream mix to the top of the cake.

Serve.

Nutrition

Calories: 350

Carbs: 10g

Protein: 8g

Fat: 30g

Fiber: 5g

Sweet Coconut Raspberries

Preparation Time: 10 minutes
Cooking Time: 2 minutes
Servings: 12

Ingredients
1/2 cup dried raspberries
3 tbsp swerve
1/2 cup shredded coconut
1/2 cup coconut oil
1/2 cup coconut butter

Directions
Set instant pot on sauté mode.
Add coconut butter into the pot and let it melt.
Add raspberries, coconut, oil, and swerve and stir well.
Seal pot with lid and cook on high for 2 minutes.
Once done, release pressure using quick release. Remove lid.
Spread berry mixture on a parchment-lined baking tray and place in the refrigerator for 3-4 hours.
Slice and serve.

Nutrition
Calories: 101
Fat: 10.6g
Carbs: 6.2g
Sugar: 5.1g
Protein: 0.3g
Cholesterol: 0mg

Keto-Friendly Chocolate Chip Cookies

Preparation Time: 12 minutes
Cooking Time: 12 minutes
Servings: 20

Ingredients
¾ cup coconut oil
4 oz sugar-free chocolate chips
2/3 stevia
2 eggs
3 cups almond flour
½ tsp salt
½ tsp baking soda
1 tbsp vanilla extract

Directions
Combine the coconut oil and stevia in a bowl and mix well.

Add the vanilla and eggs and stir until combined.

Mix the salt, baking soda, and almond flour in a bowl and then add to the other bowl, mixing well.

Add sugar-free chocolate chips.

Form cookies on a baking tray and put into the oven (preheated to 350F).

Cool and serve.

Nutrition (per cookie)
Calories: 180
Carbs: 4g
Protein: 5g
Fiber: 2g
Fat: 20g

Delicious Berry Crunch

Preparation Time: 10 minutes
Cooking Time: 4 minutes
Servings: 2

Ingredients

2 tbsp almond flour

1 tsp cinnamon

1/2 cup pecans, chopped

2 tbsp coconut oil

1/4 tsp Xanthan gum

1/4 cup Erythritol

1 tsp vanilla

20 blackberries

Directions

Add blackberries, vanilla, erythritol, and xanthan gum into the heat-safe dish. Stir well.

Mix almond flour, cinnamon, pecans, and coconut oil and sprinkle over blackberry mixture—then cover the dish with foil.

Pour 1 cup of water into the instant pot, then place the trivet in the pot.

Place dish on top of the trivet.

Seal pot with lid and cook on high for 4 minutes.

Once done, release pressure using quick release. Remove lid.

Serve and enjoy.

Nutrition

Calories: 224

Fat: 19.8g

Carbs: 40.3g

Sugar: 33.9g

Protein: 2.9g

Cholesterol: 0mg

Keto-Friendly Chocolate Mousse

Preparation Time: 10 minutes
Cooking Time: 10 minutes
Servings: 10

Ingredients

2 cups whipping cream
½ cup stevia
½ cup cocoa
2 tsp vanilla extract
½ tsp salt

Directions

Add the whipping cream to a bowl and whisk.
Add the stevia, cocoa, vanilla extract, and salt and combine.
Serve.

Nutrition

Calories: 450
Protein: 4g
Fiber: 4g
Carbs: 12g
Fat: 45g

Keto-Friendly Cheesecake

Preparation Time: 18 minutes

Cooking Time: 50 minutes

Servings: 10

Ingredients

6 packs of 8 oz cream cheese (full fat)

1 ½ cups almond flour

2¼ cup stevia

5 eggs

8 oz sour cream

6 tbsp butter

1 tbsp vanilla extract

1 tsp cinnamon

Directions

Combine the almond flour, butter, cinnamon, and ¼ cup of stevia in a bowl.

Mix in the butter.

Pour the mixture into a springform pan and press halfway up the sides of the pan.

Refrigerate for 30 minutes.

Mix the cream cheese until fluffy and mix in the remaining stevia.

Add the eggs and beat. Add the sour cream and vanilla and mix well.

Pour the mixture into the crust and bake in the oven (preheated to 325F) for 50 minutes.

Cover and refrigerate for 10-12 hours.

Serve.

Nutrition (per slice)

Calories: 630

Protein: 18g

Carbs: 10g

Fat: 90g

Fiber: 3g

CONCLUSION

Following a keto diet is not simply a quick fix, and it is highly suggested that you follow it, intending to make it a lifelong lifestyle change. The keto diet is healthy for you and can help your body through the changes you will be experiencing as you turn 50 and older. Because you are not just cutting out carbohydrates completely from your diet, your body will still receive all the nutrients that it needs to sustain you.

The keto diet has become very popular for younger and older people alike. So, you should not have any problems finding a keto community or group that can give you the advice you need, answer your questions, and even meet up from time to time to share their experiences and well-loved keto recipes.

To find more support on the keto diet, you should join a few groups on Facebook to meet like-minded people who share your lifestyle goals and ideals. You can also look for new recipes online and in cookbooks. I like to buy a new cookbook every once in a while and play a game. I will take the cookbook, close my eyes, and flip through the pages. Whichever page my finger lands on, I will try that recipe and see how it is and make a note of what recipe I tried so that it is easy to come back to later.

You would be surprised to find out how many blogs are dedicated to creating and writing about keto-friendly recipes. I love these blogs because they often provide you with a printable recipe at the end of the blog page that details all the information about the recipe, including nutritional information. You can print out your favorite recipes like this and add them to a file to refer back to later.

If you are faced with any difficult situations when following the keto diet, you should remind yourself why you started the keto diet and what you are hoping to see from your diet health-wise or lifestyle-wise. No matter your reason for starting the keto diet, you should focus on that and try to put difficult situations behind you. If you are still having trouble coping with a certain situation, you can always ask for advice from one of your keto groups or like-minded friends. You never know, they might have some great advice for you.

Printed in Great Britain
by Amazon

13648256R00106